Cruise Ship Job In 14 Days

The LASER Strategy for Next Generation Applying

by

Bogdan Mihaylov

authorHOUSE™

1663 Liberty Drive, Suite 200
Bloomington, Indiana 47403
(800) 839-8640
www.AuthorHouse.com

This book is a work of non-fiction. Unless otherwise noted, the author and the publisher make no explicit guarantees as to the accuracy of the information contained in this book and in some cases, names of people and places have been altered to protect their privacy.

© 2005 Bogdan Mihaylov. All Rights Reserved.

No part of this book may be reproduced, stored in a retrieval system, or transmitted by any means without the written permission of the author.

First published by AuthorHouse 12/28/04

ISBN: 1-4208-1045-6 (sc)

Library of Congress Control Number: 2004098579

Printed in the United States of America
Bloomington, Indiana

This book is printed on acid-free paper.

Table of Contents

Introduction 11
Impact Cover Letter Writing 15
    The Crucial Importance of Your Mental Attitude 15
    How to Write an Impact Cover Letter 16
    How to Create Personal Uniqueness 17
    How to Market and Sell Your Skills to the Hiring Manager .. 18
    How to Project a Winning Image 19
    Use the AIDA Formula: Attention-Interest-Desire-Action 20
    How to Close the Sale 21
    The Anatomy of a Cover Letter 22
    The 9 Parts of a Cover Letter 22
    How to Handle Tough Issues 25
        How to Handle Request for Salary Expectations 26
        What If You Have No Qualifications 27
    Cover Letter Check List 28
How Exactly the Top 1% Applicants Gather Crucial Details and Immediately Stand Out 30
    Get in Demand. Become an Impact Player 30
    Do not hurry to write. Think hard first! 31
    Why Great Resumes Also Go in the Trash 31

How to Gather Crucial Details for an Outstanding Resume 31

Spend 1-2 minutes on the phone 32

What to do with Princess Cruises- the Exception 34

Stand Out, Pay $2,000-$3,100 or Forget About the Cruise Jobs 34

It Is All About Exceptional Hospitality 35

Why It Is a Cutthroat Industry for the Staff 35

Impact Resume Writing 39

Resume Strategies 39

The Focus Statement 40

What Is Your Dolarized Value 40

Are You A Perfect Match 41

Only Relevant to the Desired Job Information 41

Zero Exaggerated Facts 42

Stand Out With Accomplishments 42

Impact Resume Writing 43

    Start Writing 44

    Create Your Focus Statement 44

    Choosing the Right Resume Format 45

    Chronological Format 46

    Functional Format 46

    How to Smooth Its Disadvantages 46

Combination Format- The Best 47

Why Poor Design Will Kill Any Resume 47

    How to Balance Design and Content 48

    10 Ways to Push the Employer's Hot Buttons 48

The Anatomy of a Resume 49

Contact Information 49

    Focus Statement 49

Employment Section 50

    Start Each Sentence with an Action Verb 51

    Focus on Verifiable Accomplishments 52

Educational Section 52

    A Mistake, Which Can Screen You Out Immediately 53

    How to Distinguish Inappropriate Information 53

What If You Do Not Meet a Requirement 53

Extra Information 54

    Interests 54

    Military 54

    Awards, Honors and Recognition 55

    Technical or Computer Skills 55

Additional Advice for Outstanding Resume 55

    Why is it Crucial to Express Mail Your Application Package 56

Resume Check List 57

How to Ace an Interview 58

   The Crucial Importance of Your Attitude 58

   Common Mistake, Which Can Fail Everything 58

      Are You Interested in Promotions 59

      Use "The Ultrasound Strategy" 59

      Additional Secret for Success 60

      Be Careful with a Sneak Strategy They Use 60

      How to Survive in a Stress Interview 61

      Follow the APA Directive 61

      Immediately Follow Up with a Thank You Letter 62

Appendix A: 300 Action Verbs 63

Appendix B: Cruise Ship Employment Directory 68

   Carnival Cruise Line 68

   Princess Cruise Line 70

   Royal Caribbean Cruise Line 71

   Norwegian Cruise Line 72

   Disney Cruise Line 73

   Celebrity Cruise Line 74

   Holland America Cruise Line 76

   P&O Cruise Line 77

   Costa Cruise Line 78

Star Cruise Line 79

Seabourn Cruise Line 80

Silversea Cruise Line 81

Cunard Cruise Line 81

Radisson Cruise Line 82

Crystal Cruise Line 83

Appendix C: 128 Cruise Ship Jobs Directory 84

Deck Department 84

Engineering Department 88

Entertainment Department 93

Concessionaires 98

Medical Department 104

Hotel Department 105

F&B Department 108

Housekeeping Department 113

Culinary Department 116

Appendix D: Complete Directory Of All 73 Concessionaires' Addresses 120

Art Auctioneers 120

Beauty Salon and Spa 121

Casino Concessionaires 122

Cruise Staff 123

Deck and Engineering 124

Entertainment Agencies 125

Food & Beverage 126

Gentlemen Hosts 128

Gift Shop/Retail Sales 128

Lecturer and Instructors 128

Medical Agencies 129

Musical Floor Show Producers 129

Photography 130

Recruiting Agencies 131

Security and Firefighters 132

Introduction

Stand out, Pay $2,000-$3,100 to an agent or Forget about the cruise ship jobs. The S.P.F approach sets the three major ways in front of you. If you are interested in the **stand out highway** then you need the exclusive L.A.S.E.R strategy.

First, use the book to **locate** the most appropriate cruise line and person in charge of the hiring for your desired position. Then follow all the step-by-step instructions for writing an impact resume and cover letter in accordance with the standards set by the **Professional Association of Resume Writers** and *The Chicago Manual of Style*. Proceed with the advanced strategies from the chapter "**How Exactly the Top 1% Applicants Gather Crucial Details and Immediately Stand Out**". You will learn how to find out and fully **anticipate** the hiring manager's even unexpressed wishes and needs. When you finish, go through two, thorough checklists and you will have what I call a "Yo-yo" Cover Letter and Resume.

Whenever you roll down a yo-yo it always goes back to you. Follow this example and trash away from your mind 3 common things: "trying", "hoping" and "waiting". It is very important to set a similar state of mind that within 14 days from **express mailing** your application and **rehearsing** for the interview you will get a cruise ship job. If you really believe that a new and better life for you depends on getting a cruise ship job then agree that NO "trying, hoping or waiting" have any place in your mind set or application work. Once you learn how exactly to **stand out** and create Yo-Yo Cover Letter and Resume, which have focus and impact **express mail** them and start **rehearsing** for the interview.

Even if you know by heart the "101 Great answers to the toughest interview questions" it will take me 30 seconds or less to find out for example that you are not a positive person despite all your presentation and answers.

There are tens of thousands of candidates applying to the cruise lines and choosing the best ones have become extremely important. That is why all hiring managers are going through extensive trainings for the latest tips and tricks in the interview science.

By following very closely the tendencies in the cruise and human resources industries I can reveal you that big companies such as the major cruise lines have already started to incorporate strategies originating from such places as the CIA. If you know that it takes up to **US $10,000** to replace a leaving employee plus the notoriously high turnover in the cruise industry you can understand why mistakes-free hiring is already crucial for them!

In the chapter for "How to Ace an Interview" I will present you the advanced "ultrasound strategy". Use it to interview the interviewer and gather additional crucial information which will help you to set yourself even further apart from your competition. Plus follow "The APA Directive" so each of your answers will be the right one and will add points to your candidature.

Everything in the book has one goal- to make you stand out completely. That's why on every step on the way you will have clear instructions, goals and deadline. As a result when 14 days pass from sending your application package you will have a cruise ship job.

Frequently asked question: Are there only strategies in the book and no general-statistical information, which dominates the content of similar books?

The focus of the book is the macro L.A.S.E.R strategy and additional 6 micro ones. Away from it and especially on the accompanying web site- Cruise Ship Jobs Directory there are **141 pages** with complete information regarding cruise line's profiles, **132 cruise ships'** crew, guests, age, nationality of the crew/staff and the **most thorough descriptions** for 128 cruise ship jobs you can find anywhere.

In short, you have **3 times as much information as you can** than you can find in all the available books on getting a cruise ship job. See for yourself.

My overall work on the book and the site is also an example what you should do to get a great cruise ship job- OVER deliver both quality and quantity.

Let's continue now with the principles explained in the first chapter "Impact Cover Letter Writing" and the crucial importance of your mental attitude.

Impact Cover Letter Writing

The Crucial Importance of Your Mental Attitude

Marketing and selling yourself depend on getting noticed, standing apart, and being different from everyone else. That's why the mentality, which will guide the writing of your cover letter and resume is essential for your success during the application process.

The 95% losers keep on doing the same old things. They all send a standard cover letter and resume thinking that this is enough someone to call them. The experience proves that such attitude in 95% of the cases results in waiting, and waiting. Do you think that the cruise lines are interested in hiring ordinary people who think they are so great that will be hired for sure?

One manager describes very well this kind of mentality: "I have my degree; I am sharp; what can you do for me?" The moment a screener or a hiring manager notices such arrogant and self-centered application, he tosses it directly into the trash. Yes, directly.

They don't need great people. What they really need are applicants who place the employer's interests and needs beyond theirs. Period. They like applicants who keep on writing **you** instead of **I**.

Thousands of people coming from poor countries around the world with no experience and basic English are hired. Why? They are genuinely willing to work hard, dedicatedly and loyally for up to three contracts. Compare this with the majority of applicants who have great demands written right in their initial application and never come back for a second contract if hired.

You will be trained what and how exactly to do onboard. However nobody can change your mental attitude and understanding. That's why mentality rules and is the single most important criteria for screening out people right away. Even a simple cover letter and resume, which have average design, will attract the attention of the cruise line IF it is heavily loaded with benefits for the employer.

For example you can make more money, save time, cut costs, improve efficiency, solve problems, increase competitiveness, retain the existing and attract new guests, build valuable relationships or expand their business. If you can do such things then you will be hired. Why? The cruise lines need exactly such people who will have a strong impact on their top or bottom line and will make them more competitive within the severely competitive cruise industry.

For land-based jobs a very active and proactive approach may be pushy. However the situation regarding the cruise ship jobs is very different. You will work many hours without days off for several months. Not everyone can and want to face such challenge. That's why if a candidate makes it very clear that they really want a job and pursue it till the very end, will usually get it. Such applicant proves with actions their determination, commitment, and energy. All these qualities are in great demand in the cruise industry.

How to Write an Impact Cover Letter

Most hiring managers will read first the cover letter and then, if they are impressed, will continue with the resume. Why? It shows them in few paragraphs your intelligence, professionalism, communication skills and personality. That's why approach its writing carefully and thoughtfully because a badly written cover letter will immediately put an end to your application!

Key point is to focus on the employer's needs and concerns. This single thing will determine 99% of the final result from your application.

If they read yet another self-centered canned letter, which contains nothing red-hot relevant, your whole application package will hit the trash.

That's why your whole preparatory work should be thorough, accurate and well-researched. Start at the web site of the cruise line of your choice and learn everything about their products, services and culture. I mean really everything. In this way you will show genuine interest in becoming part of their team. Also, later you will avoid asking questions which are answered on their site.

Find specific keywords, especially in their mission statement, which best describe their most important principles and values. Then use them in your cover letter and resume. Accumulate as much as possible information from this book, its accompanying site www.cruise-ship-jobs-directory.com and the cruise line's site. Then show in your cover letter and resume how those requirements, responsibilities, expectations, values, and goals exist in your own professional and personal history.

How to Create Personal Uniqueness

You must stand out when hundreds are applying for the same job by creating personal uniqueness. Your skills and experience are a product and your cover letter and resume should market and sell them to the hiring manager who is your ultimate customer.

The super sales people completely customize any sales literature to the customer's needs and wishes. In this way they create interest and affirm the value and benefits of the product for the customer.

To end up with a winning cover letter, you have to write, rewrite, edit, and after some time edit again. Whenever you come back to it put yourself in the employer's shoes and read it from this point of view. Then when you are already in a strong position you will have a chance to state what you want and need.

Here are several questions to ask yourself every time you come back to your cover letter:

-Does it attract your attention within a few seconds?
-Does it quickly summarize how your qualifications match the requirements and why you want the job?
-Is it really intriguing enough to read it all?
-Does it answer quickly and clearly the question: "Why you are the best candidate for the position?
-Does it present your key accomplishments, experience, professionalism, and confidence?

How to Market and Sell Your Skills to the Hiring Manager

The main point in writing a cover letter and resume is to sell yourself to the prospective employer. This is what the 5% winners are doing their best to do. The only proven strategy to achieve this is to "translate" all your skills, experience, and talents into direct and indirect benefits for your boss-to-be. How? If some of your skills are able to solve a specific problem facing the employer, say so. If you have measurable achievements, which can prove that you will be of great help, present them.

The hiring manager should have the feeling that your cover letter addresses their main needs and concerns. This will be evidence that your whole application package is custom-tailored for this particular cruise line. To strengthen this impression use several times "you". Avoid using as much as you can "I", "my" and "me". However, if it is absolutely necessary incorporate them in phrases, which focus on the employer's needs. Keep on tightening this impression by selling yourself using benefits instead of writing baseless claims and demands.

Let your typical style and way of expression to flow through the text. A more conversational tone may be helpful for you and will be fine with the hiring managers. After all, one of the most important things they want to see in the cover letter is your personality. However, keep in mind that this is a formal type of correspondence. That's why cute, funny, dry or self-serving type of cover letter will be enough reason your application to be ignored.

To summarize, use formal, yet conversational style, which allows your unique personality to find its reflection on the paper. Wrap all this with systematical selling through turning every significant feature and fact from your history into benefit for the company. Then you will definitely have an impact cover letter.

How to Project a Winning Image

Carefully think what image your cover letter will form in the mind of the hiring manager. Although the details will come from the resume, here focus on presenting yourself as an educated/ experienced professional who is knowledgeable of the cruise line's products, services and needs. Then sell yourself as a perfect fit for the company's culture as well as a solution to some specific problem or concern the hiring manager may have. Then you will position yourself as an outstanding candidate because you have done your homework on the company and have anticipated in advance their main needs, concerns and questions.

Whether you are a perfect fit for a specific job will depend on your hard skills like proficiency in MS Word and Excel. On the contrary, your soft skills and work habits like team player, work well under pressure, etc. will determine how you will fit in the company.

For maximum information on this read the cruise line employment profiles as well as the complete job descriptions on the book's accompanying www.cruise-ship-jobs-directory.com

When it comes to revealing tidbits from your personality, character, or even philosophy please use your common sense and the position you are applying for. The rule of thumb is if it supports your candidature and is relevant to the job itself, include it. For example if you are applying for Sports Director and like to jog 2 days per week say so. If you love your job and can't imagine your life without it make it clear. However if you are applying for Accountant and mention your passion for budge jumps it will probably be counterproductive.

Use the AIDA Formula: Attention-Interest-Desire-Action

The whole cover letter must be based on the AIDA formula, which stands for Attention-Interest-Desire-Action. It is crucial to grab the attention of the hiring manager within 2-3 seconds. Achieve this through opening sentence, which is original quote, interesting fact, some intrigue or confident appeal. The goal is to grab the reader's attention and to generate enough interest to continue reading the body. The opening sentence is the equivalent of the "first impression". If it stands out than you have set the stage for a cover letter, which will stand out from the others.

Effective initial technique is to mention the name of a common friend, colleague or relative who is already working at the cruise line you are applying for. Very often this is enough to quickly go ahead of the other candidates. If you have a close enough acquaintance definitely ask for permission to use their name in your application.

Impact Cover Letter Writing

The next step in the AIDA formula is to create desire. How? Prove to the hiring manager that you are exactly what they are looking for. The body of the cover letter is the best place to present highlights from your most significant accomplishments and additional advantages, which will strengthen your image.

The Professional Association of Resume Writers recommends doing this with a bulleted list and measurable strong points. Regarding your soft skills if you simply state that you are a team player it will be perceived as self-serving. However, if you have some written recognition for being an "example of a team player" then include it because you can prove it.

The rule is that only measurable and proven accomplishments, skills, knowledge, etc. should go in the cover letter. Anything else, which only states something, will weaken the overall impression.

Avoid taking something from your resume and using it as it is in the cover letter. 4-5 highlights, which are reworded from your resume, will do the job. It is important to use every opportunity to present your key accomplishments and skills from various angles. In this way the hiring manager will form a vivid 3-dimentional picture of yourself as a professional and person who can really fit perfectly and do the job.

Use clear and direct way of presentation without any company terminology or lofty words, which an average person will find it difficult to understand.

How to Close the Sale

When it comes to closing the sale do it in a way which will determinately and immediately separate you from the rest. How? Offer a follow-up telephone call. Note that this is a get it or lose it factor.

If you are concerned for the cost, calm down. The cruise lines always want the call for the interview to be on their expense. The chances are that you will NOT have to call. The whole thing is entirely for the purpose of separating yourself. That's it. Just think for a second how many candidates will offer to call for scheduling a mutually agreeable time for an interview? Very few and because of this the hiring managers remember them. For example:

Perhaps a good next step is to learn more about your specific needs, Mr. Hartford. May I call on Friday, 26th to see if we can arrange a mutually agreeable time for an interview? If you would like to contact me, I can be reached on my home phone number at (555) 555-555 in the evenings or on my cell phone, anytime, at (888) 555-555.

Thank you for your time and consideration.

The Anatomy of a Cover Letter

There are three main parts:

Introduction- make it attention-grabbing, fresh and relevant.

Body- present your most significant accomplishments, range of qualifications or relevant titles and number of years experience. Also show genuine understanding of the employer's needs, and concerns.

Closing- use the confident and proactive finish, which you can find below, to immediately separate yourself from the crowd.

The 9 Parts of a Cover Letter

Contact information: list your name, address, city, state, zip, home/cell telephone and personal e-mail exactly as they are on the resume.

Use a state name as abbreviation but spell it out in the body. The department name of the hiring manager should be capitalized. Make sure that the name is a bigger size, so that it would be easy to find your resume in a pile.

Date: preferably use the date when you will send the whole application. The best days of the week to arrive on the manager's desk are Tuesday, maximum Wednesday.

Manager's address: include name, title, full cruise line name, its street address, city and zip.

Subject Line: Each hiring manager wants to know right away what position you are applying for. That's why this is the best place to state it.

A chance to separate yourself once again is also to mention where you have learnt about the open position. Examples:

Subject: Pastry Chef, Aug. 12 issue of Overseas Jobs Express

Re: Open position for Engineer on Carnival's web site

Salutation: For example: Dear Mr. Peterson:

You can find the telephone numbers of the cruise lines in their profiles in the book. Definitely use them to learn the name of the person in charge of the hiring decision for your desired position. If the name is not traditional ask for the spelling because misspelling the name will result in negative first impression. In case that you do everything possible and Human Resources refuse to give you any name use "Dear Hiring Manager".

Body: The purpose of the opening sentence is to grab the attention of the reader and create enough interest to keep reading. Then the body has to generate desire to find out more details about you in the resume. Highlight in a bulleted list maximum 5 key points, which make you a really valuable and unique applicant. Continue offering a follow up phone call.

Polite closing: Keep to the standard and use "Sincerely".

Signature: Leave three lines after "Sincerely" for your signature. The standard is to use black ink but if you cannot find such use blue ink.

Your Name: Once again it is very important throughout your application package to have consistency. That's why write your name in the same way anywhere on your cover letter and resume. If your name is William Clinton but everyone known you as Bill Clinton then use this form of your name.

Roland Bergman
2341 Sunny Str.
San Diego, CA 91405
(555) 555-555
roland-bergman@yahoo.com

March 21, 2004

Mr. Mark Hartford
Director of Human Resources
Carnival Cruise Line
3655 NW 87th Ave.
Miami, FL 33178

Re: Open position for Accountant on Carnival's web site

Dear Mr. Hartford:

Start with a bang! You have 2-3 seconds to grab the manager's attention and set the stage for outstanding cover letter.

> Continue generating interest and desire to learn more about you by answering two questions: "Why do you want the job?" and "What makes you the best candidate?
>
> List the ultimate benefits you can bring to the table as bullets. For example:
>
> ♦ Great benefit for the employer N1
> ♦ Great benefit for the employer N2
> ♦ Maximum 5 of your most significant benefits
>
> Close the sale in a strong way summarizing 2-3 significant benefits. Then offer a telephone call.
>
> Sincerely,
>
> Ronald Bergman
>
> Enclosure

Enclosure: Two lines below your name type Enclosure, so the reader will know there is another thing to review. During the initial application send only your cover letter and resume. If there is a request for additional information like references, certificates, etc. then again include your resume, the additional information and on the cover letter write- Enclosures (1x)

Post Script (P.S.) Use such only if you have really original afterthought or closing idea, which must add additional value for the employer.

How to Handle Tough Issues

Keep the content and tone of everything you write in your whole application package 100% positive. Even if you are fired at your previous job keep it for a direct type of communication as an interview. Then you have greater chances to handle it better and put a positive spin on it. Of course you should prepare in advance for anything negative in your personal and professional history. If one of the first things, which a hiring manager reads about you is "termination" your application will go directly in the trash.

Remember that during the initial screening process the aim is to reject as many applications as possible. Even a single typo, a grammar mistake, a negative word, or a fact will be more than enough reason to screen you out. That's why keep everything 100% positive and error-free if you want to make it through the first cut.

How to Handle Request for Salary Expectations

Some of the companies like Norwegian cruise line want to see your salary expectation within your initial application. Again the reason is to reject people based on this criteria. If you want more than they agree to give you the rejection is immediate.

On the contrary, if you make the mistake to state a fixed salary and it is lower than they are willing to give you then you will make yourself a bad favour.

That's why the best approach towards such requirement is to give a salary range in your cover letter. Include maximum one or two sentences. For example:

"My compensation has ranged from $500-$700 depending on performance bonuses/tips. I have a flexible position on this topic and my expectations are in line with the cruise industry standards."

Since this is a very important topic I have gone in great details about it in the Interview section. Make sure that you know everything before you write about it in your cover letter and later discuss it in an interview.

What If You Have No Qualifications

Hiring managers and recruitment specialists make it clear in all surveys that they want to know from your cover letter why you think you are qualified for the position. That is why this topic can be quite difficult for people with little or no professional experience. There are several things, which can help you to make a favorable impression.

The first one is to focus on your Educational background and if you have some internship or part time job experience. Then show how they can be of value to the employer.

Also, it is fine to present your strongest soft skills. Do your best to support them with facts. For example, if you are a great team player and you were selected for leader of the volleyball team in your college then it is a lot more convincing.

When you have little or no experience it is essential that you show a very positive, upbeat and enthusiastic image. Since the applicants' personality is of great importance in the cruise industry make sure that you will form a positive picture of yourself without exaggerating anything.

Your cover letter must show in-depth research of the cruise line. It is OK to write: "I want to work for Carnival because it is the industry leader". However if you back it up with their 40% market share and more than 8 million vacationers per year then it is a lot more serious and impressive. Why? You have spent time researching their web site and brochures to know this. This will immediately position you as a really serious and valuable candidate despite your lack of experience.

It is important to show professionalism through your cover letter and resume. Expressing willingness to learn as well as positive and enthusiastic attitude have value and are some of the qualities, which are in great demand in the cruise industry.

In addition, follow all pieces of advice for employer's focus and proactive attitude towards the phone call for an interview and you will definitely stand out.

Cover Letter Check List

The following checklist consists of 20 questions, which perfectly summarize the most important dos and donts of cover letter writing and design. Use it after you finish and even before this.

- ☐ You have a cover letter.
- ☐ It is 1 page long.
- ☐ Answers: How your qualifications match the requirements for certain cruise ship job?
- ☐ Answers: Where you learnt about the open position if applicable?
- ☐ Immediately obvious that you are a good fit for the company.
- ☐ 100% focused on the employers needs and concerns.
- ☐ 100% spelling and grammar free.
- ☐ Demonstrates good writing ability.
- ☐ Contains all your contact information: name, address, home/cell phone, and personal email.
- ☐ Addressed to the hiring person.
- ☐ Contains current date, full cruise line's address, personalized salutation, impact body, sincerely, your signature in black ink, your name and enclosure.
- ☐ 100% accurate and hype-free.
- ☐ Highlights accomplishments in short bulleted list.
- ☐ You are applying for specific position.
- ☐ Doesn't contain specific salary.
- ☐ Contains only relevant to the job information.
- ☐ Formal, yet conversational tone, which reflects your personality.

- ☐ Excellent symmetry and visual balance throughout the whole letter.
- ☐ Will arrive on Tuesday.
- ☐ Offers a follow up phone call on Friday.

The next chapter is dedicated to two very important questions:

- How exactly the top 1% cruise ship applicants gather crucial details for their success?
- Why great resumes also go in the trash?

How Exactly the Top 1% Applicants Gather Crucial Details and Immediately Stand Out

Get in Demand. Become an Impact Player

In this chapter I am going to strip the whole application process from concept to hiring in front of you. This is necessary to visualize and realize that the success or failure of your application for cruise ship jobs is usually predetermined before you write a single word.

The good cruise lines are always looking for impact players. Show them you can improve their top or bottom line and you will be in demand. When a cruise line's manager hires someone the company makes an investment. It is just like buying any productivity-improving machine.

Your services are a product and the hiring manager is your customer. You will be hired if you can solve some problem (job) and your compensation is less than what the customer will earn from your work. This is the customer's expectation also known as ROI or Return on Investment. It includes your salary, benefits, food, accommodation, insurance, etc. To buy your services, he or she should feel good about you and is sure that you will do the job.

Do not hurry to write. Think hard first!

95% of the cruise line applicants are mainly worried about the writing itself of their cover letters and resumes. However, all their efforts go in the trash because they do not give their whole application campaign a serious thought in advance.

In the cruise industry you will be competing with hundreds other applicants for one position. That is why in each case what the hiring manager exactly needs and wants will determine whose services they will buy.

Why Great Resumes Also Go in the Trash

Let us suppose that you have a knock out resume in accordance with every professional rule. You read it and very impressed think:"If I were the hiring manager, I would definitely hire myself based on it". You eagerly send it to the cruise line and begin waiting. Why did it go to the trash? It is very simple. It did not show immediately the hiring authorities what they exactly wanted and needed to see in it.

In addition to having a great product you have to custom-tailor the marketing literature (your cover letter and resume) to the specific needs and wishes of the customer. Only then you have real chances to make a sell.

How to Gather Crucial Details for an Outstanding Resume

There are only three ways:

- Read the hiring manager's thoughts.
- Talk on the phone 2-3 minutes.
- Figure it out somehow.

Most probably you do not have paranormal talents, so the first drops out. The second one is recommended by all professional resume writers and career coaches. Why? All cruise lines have job lines and the human resources staff will usually help you find out who is the hiring person. Then it is easy to contact them and ask one or two questions, whose answers will tell you exactly what this person wants and needs to see in a resume. The rest is simple. Just write and design it the way they want it.

Also, it is a lot better to start your cover letter thanking them for the time on the phone. Since there is already some relationship between you, your application will go far ahead of the rest. There is a big difference between reviewing the resume of a perfect stranger and the one of somebody you have talked with.

Spend 1-2 minutes on the phone

Spending 1-2 minutes on the phone will be invaluable. Why? First, you can ask human resources are there open positions for the job you are interested in. If there isn't ask will there be in the near future. In 1 minute you can easily find out that neither now nor in the near future there will be any opportunity for you with this cruise line. You will save all the necessary work to research, write custom-tailored cover letter and resume, send them, and you know already- wait.

Otherwise you will know that now or soon there will be an opportunity to get a cruise ship job with this company. Then, the next step is to get the name, title and phone number of the hiring person. Here is an example of a preliminary phone call:

- Carnival's job line. How can I help you?
- Good morning. My name is Bogdan Mihaylov. Who am I talking with?
- Natalie Williamson, HR generalist.
- Ms. Williamson, could you tell me if you have an open position

for Waiter?
- Yes, there is one.
- Could you help me to personalize my application package? Do you know the name and title of the hiring person for this open position?
- Ms. Mary Parker, our Human Resources Director.
- Would you spell Mary?
- M-a-r-y.
- Thank you. I would like to learn also what specific requirements and expectations has Ms. Parker for this position. Is it possible to learn her phone number and call her?
- Yes, it is 555 555-555.
- May I call her now?
- She is on a meeting. Call her in two hours'.
- Thank you very much, Ms. Williamson. Have a nice day.

It is easy to ask HR 2-3 polite questions. Their job is to answer applicants' questions so use this opportunity. During the short conversation show good communicational skills because it is possible "Ms. Williamson" to receive and screen your application. That is why do your best to build rapport with the person from Human Resources. It can make the difference between receiving a lot or little help. For specific techniques for building instant rapport look at the chapter dedicated to Interview.

At some point Human Resources can refuse to give you more information. Then find out if this is company's policy or the person is not in mood and does not want to talk a lot on the phone. In the first case comply, while in the second call on the next day at a different time and talk with one of the other operators.

95% of the applicants fail before they even start writing their cover letter and resume? Why? They do not ask 1-2 questions at least to check is there an open position. The top 1% applicants check and know for sure where to focus their efforts. With additional 1-2 questions they find out what the name, title and specific requirements of the hiring manager are. The rest is simple and the result is almost guaranteed employment. Why? From the hundreds applicants this top 1% immediately stand out even before their cover letter and resume are reviewed. They know exactly:

Who is the hiring person?

What they want to read?

By spending 1-2 minutes on the phone they build a relationship and gather crucial for their success information. This practically guarantees their employment at the end. Is it worth? Definitely and the top 1% know it.

What to do with Princess Cruises- the Exception

Princess Cruises do not accept phone calls from applicants. This is another example why it is so important to know a cruise line's web site in details, so that you not make a mistake. They need only one to screen you out. Whenever you face an obstacle use the other ways of communication- fax, email, and mail. Before you start writing your cover letter you must know whom you are addressing it to. Then your whole resume must have content and design, which exactly match the requirements and expectations of the hiring manager. Otherwise you will do nothing different from those 95% applicants and the result will be expected- the trash bin.

Stand Out, Pay $2,000-$3,100 or Forget About the Cruise Jobs

It must be obvious by now that you should either stand out with your cover letter and resume or you had better save your time, efforts, and money. The other two options are to pay $2,000-$3,100 to an agent or to forget about the cruise ship jobs. I know applicants who thought they were too accomplished and experienced to call anyone and ask anything. They were "great" or "sharp" but they did not get a cruise ship job. The "great" self-centered and self-serving cover letters and resumes of "great" applicants go directly to the trash.

It Is All About Exceptional Hospitality

In the cruise ship industry it is all about exceptional hospitality. With the increasingly severe competition among the cruise lines hiring employees who can and will delight the guests is of crucial importance. Finding out the name and requirements of the hiring manager requires an extra step. This proves that you will do the same to delight the guests onboard. The cruise lines need exactly such kind of people. A "great" person would easily say:"It is not my job", "I cannot help you", or "I do not know". However, most of the cruiseners have saved hard to afford a 1-2 week on a cruise ship. That is why their expectation is nothing but a perfect vacation.

Why It Is a Cutthroat Industry for the Staff

Companies like Costa Cruises have included in their mission statement that one of their goals is "zero defects". It is unbelievable that the average satisfaction of their more than 8 million guests per year is 98%! The other cruise lines are close behind. The standards are extremely high. I completely agree that it is a "cutthroat industry" for the staff. Guests readily fill in questionnaires and if an employee receives few negative comments they will be near termination. With severe and increasing competition among the cruise lines no one can afford to lose guests and let them spread negative comments about it to their friends, relatives, etc.

Here are examples of what some of the 5 star companies pledge to their guests:

Carnival- "exceptional vacation experiences"
Royal Caribbean- "the most outstanding vacation experience on

land or sea"
Disney- "excellent service"
Costa- "zero defects and complete guest satisfaction"
When it comes to the 6 star cruise lines everything goes one level higher:
Silversea- "Above and beyond all expectations"
Radisson- "Above and beyond service"
Crystal- "a memorable experience, which the guests will cherish forever"

As you can see the cruise lines promise exceptional experience to the guests who select them for their vacation. Who will deliver on these fantastic promises? You!

Now, let us take for example a person who applies to Royal Caribbean. In his standard cover letter he expresses his wish to work for them as a Waiter. He states that he is a good person, good professional, and will do the job. In his standard resume are listed his jobs in 3 hotels with their descriptions. The screener asks herself: "Is this applicant going to provide "the most outstanding vacation experience on land or sea" for our guests? No". So his application goes to the trash.

Now let us see what will do the same person following the L.A.S.E.R strategy. The first step is to locate the most appropriate for him 2-3 cruise lines. How? He reads the complete profiles in the book and goes to the book's accompanying www.cruise-ship-jobs-directory.com Once he knows which are the most appropriate 2-3 cruise lines, which hire people with his level of experience, skills, and accomplishments he moves to the second step- anticipation. He uses the provided example how to ask for open position for Waiter and spends 1-2 minutes on their job lines.

The result is that from the three companies only Royal Caribbean has an open position. So he continues using the example to learn the name, title and phone number of the hiring manager. In just 1-2 minutes he has confirmation for open position and the contact information of the hiring authority. He calls and again within 1-2 minutes learns exactly what are the specific requirements and expectations of the hiring manager for this position.

Then it is time for the third step- to stand out even more. How? He uses the gathered information and the A-Z guidelines in the chapters for writing impact cover letter and resume. Very easily he creates exactly what the hiring manager will immediately label as "outstanding and exactly what I am looking for". The applicant uses for "start with a bang" of his cover letter:

Dear Ms. Harrison:

Thank you very much for the time on the phone two days ago. You mentioned that anticipation with the guests' needs, energy, and teamwork will be key qualities of the perfect candidate. Anticipation with the guests' even unexpressed wishes and needs has been the constant focus of my work as a waiter for more than 2 years...

In the resume's Focus Statement positioned in the visual center on the page he will selectively highlight accomplishments and facts, which directly relate to the key requirements. In this way during the initial screening she will immediately see that he can really deliver anticipation, energy, and teamwork.

Then it is time for the forth step- express mail the application package so it will bypass the screeners, go directly to Ms. Harrison, and grab her full attention.

In the cruise industry it is common practice an applicant who stands out on paper to be hired without an interview. This is true especially for entry and line level jobs like Waiter. That is why in the example Ms. Harrison would most probably not call him, especially after they have had a short phone conversation. However, for responsible or higher in the hierarchy jobs an interview will be conducted. For a person who follows the L.A.S.E.R strategy it is the last short and easy step because the hiring manager needs little in addition to the outstanding impression, which the applicant has already created. That is why the chapter dedicated to the Interview and the corresponding "ultrasound strategy" aim to help you close the sale and get the job.

Impact Resume Writing

Strategy, writing, and design are the three crucial parts of creating a knock out resume.

Again the guiding mindset is the focus on the employer. Use the details from the short phone calls to write a custom-designed resume for each cruise line, which has or will soon have an open position for you.

Your resume is marketing literature created entirely to sell your qualifications and experience to the hiring manager. To achieve this it must contain highlights of benefits, accomplishments, and dolarized value of the product- you!

With this in mind let us see what strategies to use in answering three important questions:

Who are you?
What have you accomplished?
What is your dolarized value?

Resume Strategies

A screener or hiring manager will spend 3-5 seconds glancing at your resume. Within this time they must find out who you are, what related to the desired job skills and accomplishments you have, and what dolarized value you can bring to the cruise line. These three major questions must be immediately answered in the so-called Focus Statement.

The Focus Statement

It can be two types- Objective or Qualifications Summary. The old-fashioned, self-centered resumes all start with "Objective", which states what you want. Nowadays, in the severely competitive cruise ship job market the resumes that stand out focus on what the employer wants. Why? This immediately separates you from the 95% crowd. Also, it proves to the hiring manager that you know what hospitality is all about and you can delight the cruise line's guests.

What Is Your Dolarized Value

Ask yourself: How your desired cruise ship job creates value for the company? A sales person creates value by generating sales revenue. A maintenance person eliminates costly downtime. The housekeeper provides perfectly clean rooms, anticipates the guests' wishes and needs making them loyal to the company. As a result they return again.

Every cruise ship job has value and exists to keep and get guests. Carefully consider how the job you are targeting creates value. Then dolarize it by calculating in dollars how much you are worth to your customer. The higher dolarized value the hiring manager sees in you, the higher the probability to be hired!

How value is created- by increasing revenue, reducing costs, innovating new products and services, and creating loyal guests.

Hiring managers are always trying to evaluate each candidate's potential to create value.

Help them to choose you by dolarizing properly the economic value you can potentially deliver and include it in the Focus Statement.

Are You A Perfect Match

When you write your resume it may or may not be important whether the job you are applying for is in line with your professional history. Especially in the cruise industry hundreds of people without any experience start with entry level positions. However, it is important that the resume be focused also on the job you want! How? Follow rule N1:

Only Relevant to the Desired Job Information

Let us say that you have worked for 20 years. For this time you have changed 15 different types of jobs and now you are applying for a waiter at Carnival. Are you going to write in your resume about all those 15 jobs? No, unless you want to present yourself as a chronic job hoper who does not know what loyalty means. From all 15 jobs you should take only those, which most closely relate to the position Waiter. Anything else should be omitted.

You should highlight in your resume only information, which will present you as a good or even perfect match to the desired job.

The keyword here is "present" a mental picture of yourself and your career so far. One, which will position you as a good match for the particular job and cruise line.

Hiring managers and recruiters keep on saying in surveys that one of the first things they look for is "relevant experience", or at least knowledge. If during the initial screening of your resume they see: Fire fighter, Hot dog seller, Retailer, and Bellman you will be screened out immediately. This kind of honest applicants do not make it even through the first cut. Learn from their mistakes. Make sure that the picture of yourself you will paint in the manager's mind will be red-hot relevant to the job.

One of the problems with the human beings is that they like to go from one extreme into another. That is why very common reason for immediate rejection is- hype. So we reached rule N2:

Zero Exaggerated Facts

I know how tempting can be to exaggerate one fact or another in your resume. I know and how unbelievably good and experienced are the screeners in recognizing exaggerations and hype.

That is why to be smart, yet honest is of crucial importance. The Professional Association of Resume Writer refers to this as "painting the picture you want someone to see while remaining in the realm of reality".

Even if the hiring manager has a doubt that you have exaggerated something this may easily doom your application. Why? Qualities like honesty, reliability, and loyalty are highly praised because they cannot be taught like many job functions.

That is why personality and qualities are decisive. It is much better to have an even modest resume, which demonstrates benefits and value to the employer, instead of an exaggerated resume, which will immediately go to the trash.

Stand Out With Accomplishments

When competing with hundreds other candidates for a single position you must immediately separate yourself from the rest. How? Present the scope of your experience/education, and highlight your measurable accomplishments and successes using bulleted lists. The following questions will help you with this:

- What awards, honors, and recognition have you won?
- What measurable accomplishments have you delivered for your employers?
- What significant talents and personal qualities do you have, which separate you from the rest?
- What professional qualifications, skills, and certificates have you achieved?

In addition to writing what you did, it is very important how well you did it?

Now let us continue with the second step in the process.

Impact Resume Writing

First compile the raw information you will need for the writing process. Concentrate on the accumulation of a lot of details, which you will edit and organize later on. If your cover letter is ready then copy the header, which already includes your contact information.

Proceed with your professional experience. List all your employers with dates, locations, and titles. Briefly describe how big and successful is each of the companies, your achievements and responsibilities at each of your jobs.

Next is your educational background. List your degrees, professional certificates, licenses, courses, and continuing education. GPA above 3.0 is good accomplishment. If you have attended a college then leave the high school. Otherwise provide the information about it- name, location, and dates of attendance. Continue with a full list of your skills, which are related to the job you want.

Finally think about extra information such as:

Honors, awards, recognition
Computer and technology skills
Foreign languages
International-onboard experience

Start Writing

Once you have all the raw information you can start writing. The rule of thumb is the most significant, current, and relevant information goes in the beginning.

Below your contact information is the so-called "visual center of the page". The hiring manager will directly focus on this part of your resume first. That is why it must immediately present your Focus Statement, which answers: who you are, what related to the desired job skills and accomplishments you have, and what dolarized value you can bring to the cruise line.

An old-fashioned, self-centered "Objective" will hurt your chances to stand out. That is why avoid using such.

Create Your Focus Statement

How you name this crucial and attention-grabbing part is important. Here is a list of alternative names:

Focus Statement
Expertise
Skills Summary
Professional Qualifications
Key Features
Accomplishments
Career Summary
Qualifications Profile
Highlights

or some combination from above.

Take you time to think what key points will dominate in the visual center of your resume.

If they are accomplishments opt for "Accomplishments". If you are applying for a technical job, which requires proficiency in many softwares, hardwares, etc. consider a "Skills Summary". In case there are various key points then use one of the more general "Highlights" or "Qualifications". If you have a lot of experience consider "Career Summary", or "Expertise".

The Focus Statement must answer immediately:

What experience and skills do you bring to the table that will enhance and contribute to the cruise line?

What benefits (dolarized value) will receive the employer in return for employing you?

Use these two questions to write 2-3 short and clear sentences. Make sure that they are 100% relevant to the job you are applying for, and its name is mentioned.

Choosing the Right Resume Format

There are three main formats. What will determine your choice? Do you have a stable professional history, which is in line with the desired job? If the answer is yes, then opt for a chronological resume. It is very well accepted by the hiring managers.

On the contrary, if you have big gaps, irrelevant to the desired jobs, long periods of unemployment, or you are a recent graduate then opt for a functional format.

The best is a combination, which takes the greatest advantages from both of them. Regardless of what resume type you choose, focus your resume on the exact requirements and expectations of the hiring manager and the cruise line. Now let us see the details about each resume type.

Chronological Format

The majority of hiring authorities consider it as the preferred format because it demonstrates continuous and upward career growth. The chronological type lists your positions in a progressive sequence. That is why start with the most recent one and work backward. In this way you can emphasize your stable and progressive employment history. Under each job listing include specific, measurable accomplishments, skills needed to do the job, and short description of anything significant for the company itself. This format allows you to focus the manager's attention on your accomplishments, job continuity, advancement, and growth.

Functional Format

Here the focus is exactly the opposite. Important is what and how well you did, while deemphasizing when and where you did them. Stress heavily on accomplishments, skills, qualifications, abilities, certificates, etc. but avoid correlating them to specific employer. As you can see this type of presentation creates suspiciousness what is the reason to omit the dates, titles, and employment track. Make sure that you really have a good reason to use this format. Such can be career change, long unemployment, many jobs in short time, or being a recent graduate.

How to Smooth Its Disadvantages

To smooth the disadvantages of this format after you present your strong points list key employers or such, which relate to some extent to your desired job. Since it will look as a small chronological section think for a while what to include and what to omit. For example, if you have big gaps of unemployment then omit the dates, but list the employers, and your titles. If you are a recent graduate after the Focus Statement continue with your Education section and put the focus on it. In case of career change make sure to provide short description of your previous employers. Include industry, type of business, financial and (inter) national scope of their operations.

Combination Format- The Best

If you have good employment history I strongly recommend that you opt for this type. It really combines the very best of the chronological and functional, while eliminating their disadvantages. That is why it is the most powerful and effective style of presenting yourself to a prospective employer. How can you compose it? The Focus Statement from the visual center will smoothly continue in short bulleted section, which will further present your strongest points (functional section).

Promote your key credentials, qualifications and accomplishments, supported by specific highlights of your career that match the desired job and hiring manager's requirements. Then continue with your employment history (chronological section). There include detailed information pertaining to each of your relevant jobs. This chronological section must directly support and strengthen the upper functional. What is the secret of success with this format? Powerful beginning with red-hot relevant highlights of accomplishments, qualifications, etc., which the hiring manager exactly wants to see, supported by a strong employment section.

Why Poor Design Will Kill Any Resume

A resume with poor or crowded look will directly go to the trash. The screeners are judging about the quality and professionalism of your work from the cover letter and resume. That is why if one of them has low quality presentation or content they presume that you are also below their requirements and expectations. Make sure that everything, which you send to a cruise line, is attractive and easy to read.

How to Balance Design and Content

Composing an impact resume depends on balancing both design and content. Each one of them is important for the final effect and presentation. The design is the physical layout of the information. For best results it must be simple, neat, well-organized and visually attractive. Design your resume for maximum readability, so that it is easy for the manager to locate immediately the key information, which match their specific requirements and expectations.

Note that white space, bulleted lists, bold, italic, and capitalization play an important role in distinguishing and emphasizing key details in your resume.

During the initial 2-3 seconds screening of your resume, the hiring manager should see that you are **the** perfect person. That is why your key accomplishments, relevant experience, and qualifications, which match their specific requirements must be immediately obvious.

10 Ways to Push the Employer's Hot Buttons

A resume, which is 100% focused on the hiring manager's needs, concerns, and expectations immediately stands out. To project even better image and higher dolarized value give specific examples how you can also:

- **make more money**
- **save time**
- **cut costs**
- **improve efficiency**
- **solve problems**
- **increase competitiveness**
- **retain existing and attract new guests**

- **build valuable relationships**
- **expand their business**

Keep focused on showing such benefits and value to the hiring manager and you will be hired because they badly need such people. No matter what particular job you are applying for, it creates value for the cruise line. You must focus your entire resume and cover letter on how good you are in overdelivering this value.

Now let us continue with the different parts, which make one resume.

The Anatomy of a Resume

There are 5 primary sections, which make a successful resume. They are:

1. Contact Information
2. Focus Statement
3. Employment
4. Education
5. Extra Information

Contact Information

Make sure that it matches exactly the cover letter. This conveys consistency and professionalism, which are of great importance. Do not include a work phone because hiring managers consider it dealing with personal issues during work time. Since space is limited you can reduce the font size for your contact information and present it on 1-2 lines using a bullet symbol for separator.

Focus Statement

This is the most important part of your resume! Make sure that it immediately answers:

- What job you are applying for.
- What benefits and dolarized value you can bring to the cruise line.
- What measurable accomplishments, qualities, qualifications, etc. you have that match precisely the hiring manager's requirements and expectations and prove that you can deliver on them.

How to Further Strengthen it

Graphically close it up and down with lines.

If you list many skills, use a box for additional impact. The goal is the final result to be visually attractive and guide the hiring manager's eyes immediately there.

Employment Section

Despite your choice of format the employment section is important for the hiring managers. Why? It highlights your professional career so far and emphasizes experience, qualifications, and achievements. Usually it starts with your current or most recent employer and lists backward the previous ones. For each of them include the following information:

- Name of company
- City and state/country where you worked
- Dates of employment
- Title of your position(s)

If you are using a chronological or combination format provide specific details for each employer and job you have performed. If a company is not well-known, then provide specific and significant information about it. When you are presenting each job focus on three things:

- Specific, and measurable accomplishments
- Special skills necessary to perform it
- Key responsibilities and how well you did them

Your job descriptions must be short, and focused.

Start Each Sentence with an Action Verb

To help you write short and impact sentences I have included a list of 300 Action Verbs in Appendix A. How to use them? Take a pen and notebook and start reading them slowly. Think carefully how each of these verbs can relate to your accomplishments, qualifications and career. When you finish with them, you should have at least 10 short and impact sentences. Why are they so important? Compare the following two examples:

1. I was responsible for the supervision of the day-to-day operations within the department.
2. "Supervised department of 56 employees in a fast-paced environment ensuring consistent product and service compliance with the hotel's very high standards.

The first example contains "I", which is unacceptable! Also, "I was responsible for…" is a cliché, which says nothing but consumes a lot of valuable space. Third, the whole sentence is a statement, which does not sell even one accomplishment to the hiring manager.

The second example starts immediately with the action verb supervise. It immediately focuses on selling measurable accomplishments- department with 56 employees, fast-paced environment, and very high standards. When you see a sentence, which starts with action verb and contains $, %, numbers, or verifiable facts, it immediately stands out and sells you successfully to the hiring manager. Otherwise, it is just a boring statement, which tells something to the employer.

They need only few such sentences to ignore your resume.

Focus on Verifiable Accomplishments

Focus the employment section on specific and verifiable accomplishments, achievements, and contributions. They must relate directly to the specific requirements and expectations of the hiring manager.

Briefly describe what specific skills you have used in each of your jobs. Technical, computer, communicational, problem-solving, and organizational skills are good selling points. Remember also the ten areas, which push the hot buttons of every hiring manager- making more money, saving costs, improving efficiency, etc.

Let the words you choose reflect your professionalism, energy, enthusiasm, and determination. They must prove the hiring manager that you can and will fulfill their promise to the guests for exceptional experience and time onboard.

In case that you are using a functional format present for each company- name, city, state/country, dates of employment, and title(s). That is all.

Educational Section

Present your highest degree first and if you have additional, list them backwards. This section should appear first after the Focus Statement if you have limited work experience. In such case concentrate on your achievements at school. Good selling points are GPA above 3.0, class rankings, honors and awards, scholarships, special theses and dissertations, internships, and extracurricular activities. Valued are also volunteer work and tutoring. Think carefully what is relevant to include it in your resume.

The hiring managers are mainly interested in your highest educational degree. That is why if you have a college do not include details about your high school. Otherwise give its name, city, state/country, and dates of attendance.

A Mistake, Which Can Screen You Out Immediately

The educational section can not only contribute a lot to an excellent overall impression of you, but also to spoil it. For example, you can list few colleges and many courses but without having a degree. In your eyes this can be significant, but most managers will consider it as a lack of consistency and determination to finish something you have started. Problem #1 of the cruise lines is the constant turnover. That is why even the slightest sign that you are not reliable and serious about finishing at least one contract will screen you out immediately. Again, look absolutely everything from employer's perspective.

How to Distinguish Inappropriate Information

To help you deal better with questionable topics and details ask yourself the following question: Will this information seriously increase my chances to get an interview? If the answer is no, leave it.

At some point you can look at your resume and have the feeling that you are lacking significant accomplishments and facts from your professional and personal life. In such case demonstrate high energy, enthusiasm, and determination to give 200 percent. If you face a weakness think for a corresponding strength(s), which will compensate it.

What If You Do Not Meet a Requirement

If an employer wants Bachelor's degree and you have only Associate degree then accent on areas of your experience and education where you have proven yourself and they will stand out in your resume. The requirements for each of the 128 cruise ship jobs in Appendix C are relatively flexible. The screeners will never pass on an application, which does not fit with a job description. However, hiring managers especially in the cruise industry are specialists in adapting talent to a particular job. This is yet another reason why your application must go directly to the hiring manager.

Whenever you face a weakness it is important to honestly address it by demonstrating impressive strengths and skills. Do not ever try to foul or mislead a hiring manager because sooner or later everything will be exposed. Remember also that your cover letter and resume must be 100% positive and present you in the best possible way. Save any information such as termination for an interview because only then you have chances to get over it. You have to be in a strong position to address any weaknesses and the most appropriate time for this is the interview.

Extra Information

If you include such section it must be very short and relevant to the desired job.

Interests

If you have special interests, which match the job requirements, skills, or activities then you can include them. If your targeted job is competitive or team-oriented and you are practicing some sport, which requires competitiveness or team spirit, mention it. A rule of thumb is to keep such information on one line. This is enough to give the hiring manager a good idea who you are outside the workplace.

Military

If you have been in the military to service your country and achieved an honorable discharge then you may mention it briefly. Important point is to translate military jargon into easy to understand English. If you are not sure about civil equivalents then ask for help.

Awards, Honors and Recognition

If you have such then place them in a separate section in your resume. They will be specific proves for accomplishments, which you present.

Technical or Computer Skills

If your desired job requires specific technical skills or knowledge of softwares and hardwares then present then in a separate section. The best way to list such information is in a bulleted list so that it will stand out.

Additional Advice for Outstanding Resume

The first thing, which screeners and hiring managers see from an applicant is their application package. They will judge for your professionalism and punctuality entirely by your resume and cover letter. How they look and what impression they create will determine whether they will go to the trash or not. When you finish your work, make sure there are no spots or dots made by the printer. Use laser printer and white paper of high quality. The envelope must be a big one, so you can place the papers without folding them. The only way to skip the screeners is to address it directly to the hiring manager. That is why spending few minutes on the phone will guarantee you this priceless information. You can also learn additional procedures and rules, which you have to follow.

Why is it Crucial to Express Mail Your Application Package

It may take a cruise line weeks to receive your application package. It is possible to get lost on the way, or to arrive damaged. Then it will be yet another envelope in a huge pile. However, when and who will first read your cover letter will be out of your control. This is a risk, which is not worth taking.

95% of the applicants believe that it takes months and some mass mailings to get noticed and reach an interview. This is very far from the truth. You can get a cruise ship job within 5 days from express mailing your cover letter. Whether it is FedEx, EMS, Aramex, or some other service they will professionally package your big envelope and make it attention- grabbing. Plus once you know the name of the hiring manager it will go directly to them and will immediately receive full attention. Such outstanding start is exactly what your application package needs. Then the hiring manager will open it and remember from the cover letter about you. In addition to spending 1-2 minutes on the phone, you have followed up with express mail and custom-tailored resume, which exactly matches their requirements and expectations.

Applicants who do so many extra steps and position themselves in such an outstanding way are usually hired without any additional phone conversation. At the time you send your application you can precisely tell what will follow- success or the trash bin. You have several tools outlined in the book to present and deliver your cover letter and resume in the most outstanding way in front of the hiring manger. Use all of them and you will definitely get your desired cruise job.

Resume Check List

- ☐ Related experience/knowledge is immediately evident in the resume.
- ☐ Grabs the manager's attention by matching their specific requirements and expectations.
- ☐ Only (assistant) managers can spread on 2 pages long resume. The rest have 1 page.
- ☐ Contains relevant keywords- titles, degrees, qualifications, certificates, and skills.
- ☐ Benefits loaded and graphically accented Focus Statement.
- ☐ Contains your highest degree.
- ☐ 100% accurate and error-free
- ☐ Your key selling points are quickly and easily noticeable.
- ☐ 100% employer focused
- ☐ Neat, well-organized, and visually attractive
- ☐ Contains full contact information: name, address, home/cell phone, and personal email, which match the cover letter.
- ☐ Provides measurable accomplishments, achievements and contributions in bulleted lists.

How to Ace an Interview

The Crucial Importance of Your Attitude

Treat the interview as a sales call. Your services are the product, which the hiring manager, your ultimate customer, wants to buy. The interviewer's job is to determine whether the cruise line should make an investment and hire you. What is your job? To convince the hiring manager that you are worth more than their investment in you. At the end of the month it is the salary for you and the profit for the company. Eventually, everything boils down to business for both sides.

Common Mistake, Which Can Fail Everything

If you are on the phone talking with the hiring manager, it is not over yet. The focus on the employer is necessary to be 100% because of the specific nature of the cruise industry. If you state demands and you are not flexible or understanding you will definitely lose the sale. A part of your conversation will be for your salary. Note that in most cases the hiring manager will want to hear your agreement with a fixed basic salary. In addition you may have tips, percentages, bonuses, etc.

When you see in the job description income range $1,200-$2,400 and you face a request for $200 salary do not be shocked. In this case the main part of your income will come from tips, performance bonuses, or percentage. That is why my strong recommendation is that you accept the "basic salary", which will satisfy the hiring manager. Focus on the big picture. There are hundreds of employees on the cruise ships with $100 basic salary, which are making thousands every month. Will you reject such opportunity because of $100-$200 difference in your basic salary? In this mechanism is incorporated the main reason why and how the cruise lines are achieving such phenomenal guest satisfaction. When up to 95% of your income is coming from tips, percentage on sales, etc. you will really do your best for the guests. Think about it for a while and you will see that this is fair and make sense. If you are very good and the income from an entry level position is not enough for you, remember also that there are constant promotions.

Are You Interested in Promotions

This question is very often asked. The aim is to see if they can rely on you once there is an open position in the hierarchy. Definitely answer positively. Whether you will use such opportunity or not is something you can decide once onboard. Usually the income potential from a higher position is better, so it is worth considering such opportunity.

Use "The Ultrasound Strategy"

It is a myth that during the interview you should only answer questions and ask something only if the interviewer gives you a chance in the end.

How did you learn the name, title, specific requirements, and expectation of the hiring manager? By asking in advance.

Take for example the nature's leaders in orientation and navigation- the bats. They are continuously emitting ultrasounds, which reflect in the surroundings and come back to them. By carefully listening this audio feedback they navigate perfectly even in the most complex environment, while maintaining very high speed. Follow the same strategy and conduct a preplanned and practiced needs analyze by asking careful and thoughtful questions. Prepare them in advance and practice asking them.

Additional Secret for Success

During the interview listen carefully and take notes. The secret to success is to learn for a problem or concern the hiring manager has and to present yourself as the perfect solution. Let us say that while using the ultrasound strategy, you find out that the employer is facing a big turnover. This is typical for some departments such as Pursers/Front Desk. Stressing on your loyalty and determination to stay there will calm down the manager's concern. What is the point to hire a great applicant who will soon transfer in another department or leave in 2 months? That is why it is a must to find out what difficulties is facing the hiring manager addressing them directly and determinately. It is a tough industry and they all have challenges and problems. This is your chance to prove once again that you are levels beyond the others by finding out and addressing the hiring manager's problems and challenges.

Be Careful with a Sneak Strategy They Use

Make sure that you take notes and remember your answers. Some part of the interview will contain the so-called behavioral questions. Their purpose is to give the manager two types of information:

- What will you do in a certain situation?
- Have you been telling the truth so far?

To avoid saying contradictions it is very important to know in advance exactly what image you are presenting from your cover letter and resume. If the three qualities, which characterize you are positive, energetical, and guest-focused everything you say must support this image. Before saying anything, especially how you are going to react in a certain situation think for an answer, which supports your image and qualities. Otherwise your answer will ruin all your efforts so far and the manager will lose faith in you.

How to Survive in a Stress Interview

If you read in the job description "work well under pressure", you should expect that the hiring manager will suddenly change dramatically the tone and type of questions. Let us say that you are applying for a waiter and at some point during the interview he places you in the following situation. While you are approaching the table of 6 VIP guests caring their meal you stumble and the tray falls splashing soup all over them. Furious, they jump from their seats and shout that they want to speak with the highest ranking manager. What will you do?

With this single question he can test several claims in your cover letter and resume such as being always positive, energetical, guest focused, etc. If you say that you will hide and start crying, forget about all your claims. Otherwise if your answer clearly demonstrates all these qualities then the hiring manager will believe you.

You can be sure that the hiring manager will do everything to test and approach each of your significant claims determined to find out the truth. Be honest, yet smart in what you are writing and later on saying and always keep in your mind the image you are painting for yourself right from the beginning.

Follow the APA Directive

Even if the hiring manager presents you the horrible situation like that with the soup remember "Always Positive Answers". Say that you will immediately apologize to the guests and do your very best to calm them down and compensate them for the inconvenience. The hiring manager wants to see positive and action- oriented applicants, who are confident and determined to solve any problems they could face.

If you have been terminated then again remember "Always Positive Answers". Focus on what you have learnt from this and ensure the manager that this will not happen again. Placing a positive spin on absolutely everything is a must. Even one negative word or sentence may have disastrous effect on your chances to get the job.

Even a stress interview is just a game or tool, which you should use to prove to the hiring manager that you are levels beyond the others. Stay calm and focused on giving positive answers, which support and strengthen your image. Whenever you can, go back to the employer's problems and challenges and keep on adding accomplishments, contributions, and personal qualities, which prove that you can and want to solve them. The result will be worth it.

Immediately Follow Up with a Thank You Letter

If you get the job at the end of the interview congratulations. Otherwise there is one more way to stand out. Express mail a thank you letter within 4 hours. Keep it brief and use it to thank the manager for the time on the phone. If you feel that something has gone wrong this is the opportunity to address and turn it into advantage. Keep on doing extra steps like this until you get the job. They speak more than thousands of cover letters and resumes what a really outstanding applicant you are and how incredibly valuable can be for the cruise line. Since such candidates are very rare your cruise ship job is almost guaranteed far before 14 days have passed.

Appendix A: 300 Action Verbs

Use the following verbs to add power and impact to your cover letter and resume writing. When you are presenting your current job use them in Present tense. When you are writing about your past jobs use them in Past tense. Start as many sentences as possible with an action verb to achieve brevity and attention grabbing beginnings.

Abbreviate
Accelerate
Accentuate
Accept
Accommodate
Accomplish
Accumulate
Achieve
Acknowledge
Acquaint
Acquire
Act
Adapt
Add
Address
Adhere
Adjust

Gain
Gather
Generate
Give
Graduate
Greet
Group
Guide
Handle
Heighten
Help
Hold
Host
Identify
Ignite
Implement
Improve

Admit	Incorporate
Advance	Indicate
Advertise	Influence
Advise	Inform
Advocate	Initiate
Aid	Inspire
Aim	Instruct
Alert	Integrate
Alleviate	Interest
Amaze	Interpret
Analyze	Introduce
Answer	Invent
Anticipate	Inventory
Appeal	Invite
Appoint	Involve
Approach	Join
Approve	Lead
Arouse	Learn
Arrange	Lock
Ask	Lounge
Attain	Maintain
Audit	Manage
Avoid	Mark
Award	Market
Balance	Master
Begin	Measure
Benefit	Mediate
Blend	Minimize
Block	Modify
Boast	Monitor
Brief	Move
Bring	Multiply
Broaden	Narrow
Budget	Navigate
Build	Negotiate
Call	Notify
Calm	Obtain

Capture	Open
Care	Operate
Cary	Optimize
Cater	Order
Cause	Organize
Caution	Outline
Celebrate	Overcome
Certify	Participate
Change	Perceive
Check	Perform
Circulate	Pioneer
Clarify	Place
Clean	Plan
Clear	Point
Close	Prepare
Coach	Present
Collaborate	Preserve
Collect	Print
Comfort	Prioritize
Commit	Process
Communicate	Produce
Compare	Profit
Complete	Program
Comply	Progress
Conduct	Propose
Confirm	Provide
Consider	Push
Consolidate	Raise
Consult	Rank
Contract	Reach
Contribute	Receive
Control	Recognize
Convince	Recommend
Coordinate	Record
Correct	Recover
Counteract	Reduce
Create	Register

Critique
Cut
Deal
Decrease
Dedicate
Deliver
Demonstrate
Describe
Detect
Develop
Devote
Discuss
Display
Dispose
Dissolve
Distribute
Document
Double
Earn
Ease
Economize
Edit
Educate
Elaborate
Eliminate
Empower
Enable
Encourage
End
Enforce
Engage
Enhance
Enlarge
Enrich
Ensure
Enter
Equip

Release
Relieve
Rely
Remain
Remodel
Reorganize
Repair
Reply
Represent
Request
Retain
Return
Reverse
Rotate
Safeguard
Scan
Schedule
Secure
Sell
Sequence
Set
Shape
Sharpen
Shorten
Show
Solicit
Solve
Speak
Specify
Speed
Stimulate
Streamline
Stretch
Study
Submit
Succeed
Supervise

Establish	Supply
Examine	Support
Exceed	Surpass
Expand	Systemize
Experience	Teach
Explain	Test
Extent	Thrive
Facilitate	Train
Factor	Travel
Familiarize	Triple
Fight	Turn
File	Type
Find	Undertake
Finish	Unify
Fix	Upgrade
Focus	Urge
Follow	Use
Forecast	Value
Form	Verify
Forward	Voice
Foster	Volunteer
Fulfill	Win

Appendix B: Cruise Ship Employment Directory

Below each cruise line's profile there is a directory of all its ships. You can learn their names, number of the crew and guests, age and size.

Legend: S-small (yacht-like), L-bigger, M-medium, XL-very big
O-old, M-medium age, N-new, F-future ship

Carnival Cruise Line
3655 NW. 87th Avenue
Miami, FL 33178 USA
Tel:+1 305-599-2600
Fax:+1 305 406-4700
www.carnival.com

"The Most Popular Cruise Vacation in the World!" prides itself for being the pacesetter in the whole cruise industry. Whether it is the dining experience, the fun or any other onboard activity, they always strive for "the best". Moreover with 40% market share they have definitely conquered the minds and hearts of the most cruise vacationers. If you want to work on one of the "fun ships", a positive and hard-working personality is a must.

In their mission statement they aim "to deliver exceptional vacation experiences through the world's best-known cruise brands that cater to a variety of different lifestyles and budgets, all at an outstanding value unrivaled on land or at sea".

That's why only excellent candidates can and will have the pleasure to delight Carnival's guests. The experience for you will be impressive and memorable, yet expect the money and amount of work there also to be significant. As a multi-billion company, owner of 12 other cruise lines, Carnival is the define leader you can be only pride to work for.

Name	Crew	Guests	Age/Size
Carnival Conquest	1200	2833	N/XL
Carnival Destiny	1050	2666	M/XL
Carnival Glory	1160	2833	N/XL
Carnival Legend	930	2120	N/L
Carnival Liberty	1160	2974	F/XL
Carnival Miracle	1000	2124	F/XL
Carnival Pride	1000	2120	N/XL
Carnival Spirit	930	2120	N/XL
Carnival Triumph	1150	2672	M/XL
Carnival Valor	1160	2974	F/XL
Carnival Victory	1150	2672	N/XL
Celebration	670	1486	O/L
Ecstasy	920	2052	O/XL
Elation	920	2052	M/XL
Fantasy	920	2052	O/L
Fascination	920	2052	O/L
Holiday	660	1452	O/L
Imagination	920	2052	O/L

Inspiration	920	2052	M/L
Jubilee	670	1486	O/L
Paradise	920	2052	M/L
Sensation	920	2052	O/L

Princess Cruise Line
24844 Avenue Rockefeller
Santa Clara, CA 91355, USA
They don't want calls!
Fax:+1 661-753-0133
http://employment.princess.com

One of the leading cruise lines in the industry is expanding at an unbelievable pace. Affordable luxury and "personal choice cruising" define their zealous strive for anticipation with the guests' needs and wishes even before they step onboard. That's why stress heavily how great you are in totally exceeding the expectations of the guests and what extras you can do to make their vacation truly outstanding.

You can really see the world working for Princess as they have the greatest number of destinations. Will you be happy working for them? Most probably, because they have the highest level of returning staff in the industry. This is one of their remarkable achievements.

The reason can be found in their "promote from within" policy and excellent training programs. They ensure that everything onboard is running smoothly. Also "every effort possible is made to offer the crewmembers an enjoyable environment and a rewarding career". A great company and experience, which make Princess a definite top choice for every serious about working on cruise ship.

Name	Crew	Guests	Age/Size

Caribbean Princess	1300	3100	N/XL
Coral Princess	900	1950	N/XL
Dawn Princess	900	1950	M/XL
Diamond Princess	1100	2670	N/XL
Golden Princess	1100	2600	N/XL
Grand Princess	1100	2600	M/XL
Island Princess	900	1950	N/XL
Pacific Princess	365	680	O/M
Royal Princess	515	1200	O/M
Sapphire Princess	1100	2670	N/XL
Sea Princess	900	1950	N/XL
Star Princess	1100	2600	N/XL
Sun Princess	1100	2000	N/XL
Tahitian Princess	365	680	N/M

Royal Caribbean Cruise Line
1050 Caribbean Way
Miami, FL 33132, USA
Tel:+1 305 530-0471
Fax:+1 305-539-3938
www.rccl.com

Royal Caribbean is striving to provide "the most outstanding vacation experience on land or sea". The company is one of the biggest players in the industry with substantial market share and reputation. Similar to Carnival, their programs are designed to accommodate every age and budget.

The career opportunities are excellent and the working conditions are great. The company has one of the biggest cruise ships especially those in the Voyager family. They add a mega-dimension to the work and travel experience on them. This is one of the major lines, which every candidate should consider.

Name	Crew	Guests	Age/Size
Adventure of the Seas	1185	3200	N/XL
Brilliance of the Seas	845	2400	N/XL
Empress of the Seas	685	1890	O/L
Enchantment of Seas	760	2350	M/XL
Explorer of the Seas	1180	3114	N/XL
Grandeur of the Seas	760	2350	M/XL
Jewel of the Seas	855	2500	N/XL
Legend of the Seas	735	2100	O/L
Majesty of the Seas	816	2350	O/XL
Mariner of the Seas	1180	3114	N/XL
Monarch of the Seas	816	2350	O/XL
Navigator of the Seas	1180	3114	N/XL
Radiance of the Seas	858	2250	N/XL
Rhapsody of the Seas	776	2350	O/M
Serenade of the Seas	855	2300	M/XL
Sovereign of the Seas	835	2260	O/XL
Splendour of the Seas	725	1956	M/L
Vision of the Seas	750	2300	M/S
Voyager of the Seas	1180	3114	M/XL

Norwegian Cruise Line
7665 Corporate Center Drive
Miami, FL 33126 USA
Tel: +1 305-436-4000
Fax: +1 305-436-4138
www.ncl.com

Major player in the industry focusing on freestyle cruising. Their strive to be excellent is evident from the high crew to guests ratio. That is why constant pampering care and service are expected from you.

The career opportunities are excellent because they have many ships, which travel worldwide. The working conditions are fine and the cruise line is an excellent starting point for those without serious job experience or knowledge.

Name	Crew	Guests	Age/Size
Norway	920	2030	O/XL
Norwegian Dawn	950	2224	N/XL
Norwegian Dream	650	1748	O/L
Norwegian Majesty	645	1462	O/L
Norwegian Sea	630	1518	O/L
Norwegian Sky	785	2400	M/XL
Norwegian Star	450	2224	O/M
Norwegian Sun	800	2400	N/XL
Norwegian Wind	645	1748	O/L
Pride of Aloha	420	2002	F/XL
Pride of America	440	2146	N/XL

Disney Cruise Line
PO Box 10165, Lake Buena Vista
FL 32830 USA
Tel:+1 407-566-7447
Fax:+1 407 566-3751
http://dcljobs.com

Prepare for magic and a lot of hard work. Disney Magic and Disney Wonder are the two ships, which the company operates in the Caribbean and the Bahamas. They strive for "excellent service" and have developed several steps and rules to achieve top guests' satisfaction.

Going there is easier than other cruise lines but it will be harder as well. If this is not a problem they offer to the crew great facilities, a private beach on their own Castaway Cay Island on the Bahamas, and many other benefits. They can really make worth the serious commitment and efforts required from you. A unique company and ships, which many people can find a great place to work at.

Name	Crew	Guests	Age/Size
Disney Magic	945	2400	M/XL
Disney Wonder	945	2400	M/XL

Celebrity Cruise Line
1050 Caribbean Way
Miami FL 33132 USA
Tel:+1 305 530-0471
Fax:+1 305 539-6168
www.celebrity.com

The most upscale among the five-star companies with even six-star ratings. The line boosts really outstanding service, cuisine, and reputation in the industry. They pay a lot of attention to every single employee. Why? They are aware that the success depends on every one who wears the "celebrity symbol".

The company's philosophy is focused on exceeding the guests' expectations while providing affordable cruising to some of the most exotic and paradise-like places on earth. Working for Celebrity means great experience, rewarding career, and having empowering philosophy. All these allow you to make a difference both for guests and colleagues. Consider it a top choice among the five-star cruise lines.

Name	Crew	Guests	Age/Size
Century	900	1750	M/L
Constellation	900	1950	N/XL
Galaxy	909	1870	M/XL
Horizon	642	1354	O/M
Infinity	999	1950	N/XL
Mercury	909	1870	M/XL
Millennium	999	1950	M/XL
Summit	900	1950	N/XL

Zenith 665 1374 O/L

Holland America Cruise Line

300 Elliot Avenue West
Seattle, WA 98119 USA
Tel:+1 206-286-3496
Fax:+1 206-298-3899
www.hollandamerica.com

Premium cruise line, which aims at the ultimate experience for each guest. They are proud of offering the biggest dinning selection in the industry, and of hiring chefs exclusively from prestigious gourmet society.

In every aspect of the cruise experience they aim at impeccable service, pampering genuine care, and comfort. Their requirements are high and it is privilege to work for Holland America. One of the leading lines, which keeps on setting new standards within the industry.

Name	Crew	Guests	Age/Size
Amsterdam	595	1200	N/L
Maasdam	580	1576	O/L
Noordam	530	1250	O/M
Oosterdam	795	1848	N/XL
Prinsendam	460	796	O/M
Rotterdam	530	1250	M/L
Ryndam	585	1576	O/L
Statendam	585	1576	O/L
Veendam	560	1266	M/L
Volendam	630	1650	M/L
Vista 4	795	1848	F/XL
Vista 5	795	1848	F/XL
Westerdam	795	1848	F/XL
Zaandam	580	1440	N/L
Zuiderdam	795	1848	N/XL

P&O Cruise Line

Richmond House, Terminus Terrace Southampton, S014 3PN, UK
Tel:+44 23 8052-5252
Fax:+44 23 8052-5253
www.pocruises.com

Elegance, pampering care, and great attention to details are few of the things, which characterize this impressive cruise line. If there is a company other than Carnival, which has succeeded in meeting and exceeding the expectations of practically every age and class level guest, this is P&O cruises.

Despite their British heritage everything is very modern and pampering just to ensure that the guests are really having the best possible vacation.

The expectations from the staff are huge and that is why only outstanding candidates usually go there. The experience for you will be great, and so should be for all the guests you are responsible for every day. Definitely great cruise line more easily accessible for those gravitating around the UK.

Name	Crew	Guests	Age/Size
Adonia	876	940	M/XL
Aurora	930	890	N/XL
Oceana	900	2000	N/XL
Oriana	760	1807	O/L

Costa Cruise Line
Costa Crociere S.p.A
Via Octobre XII, 2
16121 Genoa, Italy
Tel:+39 010 54831
Fax:+39 010 5483290
www.costacruise.com

Author's choice- the company is founded on very clearly defined philosophy. They aim at "zero defects", complete satisfaction, and unforgettable experience for the guests, which will make them loyal to the company.

It is the leader in Europe, and one of the major players in the industry. Costa strives to create the best environment for its employees who are considered the most important resource in achieving the company's vision and mission.

The hiring process is very thorough and once onboard, no effort is spared to make the experience for you as great as possible. A top level company with great future, and very prestigious presence. If you can meet or exceed their very high requirements and expectations definitely consider Costa Cruises.

Name	Crew	Guests	Age/Size
Costa Allegra	440	800	O/M
Costa Atlantica	900	2224	N/XL
Costa Classica	640	1300	O/L
Costa Europa	600	1400	O/L
Costa Fortuna	1012	2720	N/XL
Costa Magica	900	2224	N/XL
Costa Marina	400	780	O/M
Costa Mediterranea	870	2224	N/XL
Costa Romantica	640	1350	O/L

Costa Tropicale	540	1022	O/M
Costa Victoria	800	1950	M/XL

Star Cruise Line
Star Cruises Terminal, Pulau Indah
P.O Box 288 42009 Pelabuhan Klang
Selangor Darul Ehsan, Malaysia
Tel: 603 3109 2445
Fax: 603 3109 2098
www.starcruises.com

It is one of the important companies in the cruise industry. In just 10 years it has achieved results and recognition which other established lines can only dream of. The accent on a pampering service especially on the intimate and luxurious Megastars Aries and Taurus and the 1:1 ratio is really impressive and unique for the whole cruise industry.

With the newest fleet and exotic Asia-Pacific range of itineraries, this is definitely a great company to work for. The potential for career development is great because they keep on building new ships and expanding their impressive range of first-class services.

Name	Crew	Guests	Age/Size
MegaStar Aries	72	80	O/S
MegaStar Taurus	72	80	O/S
Star Pisces	810	1020	O/M
SuperStar Capricorn	420	700	N/M
SuperStar Gemini	420	800	O/M
SuperStar Leo	1450	1960	M/XL
SuperStar Virgo	1450	1960	M/XL

Seabourn Cruise Line
6100 Blue Lagoon Drive, Suit 400
Miami, FL 33126 USA
Tel:+1 305 463-3000
Fax:+1 305 463-3010
www.seabourn.com

Ultra-luxury atmosphere, intimate yachts and impeccable service distinguish this line from the rest. With such focus and ambience your experience will be one of the best possible among all lines.

Of course they hire only the best of the best. That is why if you have great accomplishments and five-star hotels or restaurants in your career then go ahead and do your best to make a smashing impression.

If you impress them then you know what it takes to delight their highly discerning guests onboard. From accommodation to salary, you will enjoy one of the very best in the cruise industry.

An employment with one of the ultra-luxury six-star cruise lines can be a long-term goal if you are not qualified at the beginning. Think about it.

Name	Crew	Guests	Age/Size
Seabourn Legend	150	212	O/S
Seabourn Pride	150	212	M/S
Seabourn Spirit	150	212	O/S

Silversea Cruise Line
110 E. Broward Blvd.
Ft. Lauderdale FL 33301, USA
Tel:+1 954 522-4499
Fax:+1 954 522-4499
www.silversea.com

Defining the elite luxury experience- going "above and beyond all expectations" to achieve the distinction of being the world's best. What more to say about this leader in the ultra-luxury class?

They keep on receiving the top awards from the authorities in the industry. Their Italian officers and European staff are the very best of the best. If you are a kind of celebrity in your field, apply straight there.

Name	Crew	Guests	Age/Size
Silver Cloud	196	296	O/M
Silver Shadow	245	389	N/M
Silver Whisper	245	389	N/M
Silver Wind	220	296	O/M

Cunard Cruise Line
6100 Blue Lagoon Drive, Suit 400
Miami, FL 33126 USA
Tel:+1 305 463-3000
Fax:+1 305 463-3010
www.cunard.com

"The most famous ocean liners in the world" offer more traditional style of cruising in the whole world. This British company caters to more sophisticated and heritage-loving travelers, although 50% are more casual guests.

The Queens- Mary 2 and Elizabeth 2 offer refined and unmatched traveling and work experience. Decent and very customer-focused personality plus anticipation with the needs of an older clientele are required there. These make Cunard the choice for those looking for more conservative and refined ambiance service.

Each of the Queens is a star by itself and is definitely a pride to work on one of them. They are six-star liners and that is why the company hires only the best.

Name	Crew	Guests	Age/Size
Caronia	395	658	O/M
Queen Elizabeth 2	1014	1782	O/XL
Queen Mary 2	1250	2720	N/XL

Radisson Cruise Line
600 Corporate Drive, Suit 410
Ft. Lauderdale, FL 33334, USA
Tel: +1 800 477-7500
www.rssc.com

"Above and beyond" service, luxury, and impeccable attention to details are typical onboard of this leader in the six-star segment. The company has a solid philosophy, which penetrates every single aspect of the service and facilities onboard of their multi-awards winning ships.

Definitely a great company which is dedicated to the growth of its employees and to provide them with "service training they can be proud of". Diversity and great attention to detail describe the working environment. The guests are the constant focus of everyone despite position and function. A truly outstanding company, which strives to set new standards within the cruise industry.

Name	Crew	Guests	Age/Size
RSS Voyager	445	700	N/XL
RSS Mariner	440	700	N/L
RSS Navigator	315	180	N/M
RSS Diamond	215	350	O/M
Paul Gauguin	204	320	M/M
Song of Flower	114	180	O/S

Crystal Cruise Line
2049 Century Park East, Suit 1400
Los Angeles, CA 90067 USA
Tel:+1 310 203-4450
Fax:+1 310 785-0011
www.crystalcruises.com

Top level line striving to provide something more than a perfect vacation. The intimate mega yachts provide really incredible experience for both guests and staff.

"Total service orientation" and compliance with the "crystal attitude" are expected from you, which separate the company within the six-star class. Year after year they keep on winning one of the top awards in the industry.

Hired are only outstanding and accomplished professionals who can go "above and beyond" in providing services and information of unmatched level to their discerning and experienced guests.

Name	Crew	Guests	Age/Size
Crystal Harmony	545	957	O/L
Crystal Serenity	620	1080	N/L
Crystal Symphony	545	960	M/L

Appendix C:
128 Cruise Ship Jobs Directory

This appendix contains 128 cruise ship jobs presented with their requirements and responsibilities. The complete descriptions are on the accompanying www.cruise-ship-jobs-directory.com due to limitations in the length of the book. In their full form most are 1-2 pages long. Use them to gather a lot of details, which will be very helpful while writing your cover letter and resume.

Since there are serious differences from one cruise line to another use the descriptions to get only an overview. To avoid redundancy the requirements and responsibilities are build upon each other starting from the line jobs up to the executive positions. That is why read all descriptions within a department of interest for you.

Note that the income range corresponding to each job includes salary, tips, bonuses, commissions, etc. If you have to negotiate your basic salary don't use a range provided in the book because it reflects your overall income potential per month.

Deck Department

Captain ($5,500-$10,000)
Captain's license with 20+ years experience. Certificates and

graduation diploma from a recognized maritime school or facility. Extensive knowledge of all ship navigation, maritime law and safety procedures.

Steer and operate the cruise ship using radio, radar, buoys, depth finder, lights, and lighthouses. Maintain records of daily activities, ports-of-call, and prepare progress and personnel reports. Compute position, set course, and determine speed, using charts, compass, area plotting sheets, and sextant.

Staff Captain ($4,500-$7,500)
10+ years as a staff captain. Certificates and graduation diploma from accredited maritime school or facility. In-depth experience in navigating the vessel. Dealing with all computerized and electronic equipment in the control room.

2nd in command on the vessel. Head of Deck department. In charge for external and interior maintenance, deck work, safety, security and discipline.

Chief Officer ($3,500-$4,500)
At least 3-5 years experience in a secondary position. All necessary certificates from a recognized maritime school or facility; Captain's license preferred.

Supervise the maintenance, cleanliness, and any refurbishing work together with Engineering department and the Hotel Manager. Arrange for new supplies from water and fuel.

1st - 3rd Officer ($2,000-$3,500)
Supervise and coordinate activities of crew aboard the ship. Steer vessel, utilizing navigation devices such as compass, sextant, and navigational aids such as buoys and lighthouses. Determine geographical position of ship, using loran and azimuths of celestial bodies. Supervise crew in repair or replacement of defective vessel gear and equipment. Supervise deck activities of crew.

Environmental Officer ($3,000-$6,000)
College diploma with major in Environmental Science. Onboard or closely related experience. Excellent communication and reporting skills.

In charge of protection of the environment. Ensure follow through of international and local guidelines for pollution control.

Chief Radio Officer ($2,500-$3,000)
Graduation diploma from accredited maritime school plus all applicable certificates. In-depth experience in all computerized and electronic equipment for navigation. Operate and maintain radiotelegraph and radiotelephone equipment and accessories aboard ship. Turn on power to activate generator, and throw switches to cut in transmitters and antennas. Turn dials to obtain sending frequency and volume. Receive and transmit messages following procedure prescribed by federal regulations. Maintain log of transmitted and received messages.

Safety Officer ($2,500-$3,000)
Experience with onboard safety training.

Responsible to train the crew in all safety procedures at sea. Supervise the weekly drills. Regular inspections for fire safety compliance.

Chief Security Officer ($2,500-$3,500)
Experienced professional with military background. Knowledge and experience in bomb disposal and anti-terrorism training are definite plus.

In charge of all safety issues on the ship including drills, evacuations and training as per guidelines. Responsible for all security issues on board including ship's access. Enforce fire and drug free environment.

Security Officer ($2,000-$2,500)

Extensive experience in a security position plus knowledge of firearms. Preferred candidates are with military background.

Security Personnel ($1,500-$2,000)
Experience in a security position plus knowledge of firearms. Military background is a plus.

Quarter Master ($2,000-$3,000)
At least 1-2 years experience at such secondary position onboard. Preferred are graduates from accredited maritime school.

Steer ship under direction of the Captain, navigating officer, or direct helmsman to steer following designated course. Stand by wheel when ship is on automatic pilot and verify accuracy of course by comparing with magnetic compass. Relay specified signals to ships in vicinity, using visual signaling devices such as blinker light and semaphore.

Able Seaman ($800-$1,300)
Required experience or apprenticeship/training.

Measure depth of water in shallow or unfamiliar waters using leadline. Relay specified signals to ships in vicinity using visual signaling devices such as blinker light and semaphore. Stand by wheel when ship is on automatic pilot and verify accuracy of course by comparing with magnetic compass. Steer ship under direction of ship's commander, navigating officer, or direct helmsman to steer.

Ordinary Seaman ($800-$1,300)
Required experience or apprenticeship/training.

Examine machinery for specified pressure and flow of lubricants. Read pressure and temperature displays, and record data in engineering log. Assist engineers in overhauling and adjusting machinery. Turn wheel while observing a compass to maintain ship on course. Record data in ship's log such as distance traveled and weather conditions. Paint or varnish decks, superstructures, and lifeboats.

Engineering Department

Chief Engineer ($4,500-$8,000)
Graduate of accredited maritime school. Extensive 5-8 years experience in a similar position onboard. In-depth knowledge of the engineering aspects of maritime shipping. Possess all appropriate certificates and licenses.

Direct activities of engineers engaged in preparing designs and plans to construct, enlarge, and modify certain facilities onboard. Plan and direct activities concerned with water utility systems installation, maintenance operation, and service. Provide engineering and technical direction for planning and design of water utility projects.

Asst. Chief Engineer ($4,000-$5,500)
Graduation diploma plus all necessary certificates and licenses from accredited maritime school. At least 2-3 years extensive experience at a similar position onboard. In-depth knowledge of all aspects of maritime ships engineering.

Second in charge in the Engineering department. Directs the engine staff and ensures compliance with all Company's engine-related guidelines and procedures.

1st Engineer ($3,000-$4,000)
Supervise and coordinate activities of crew engaged in operating and maintaining engines, boilers, deck machinery, and electrical, sanitary, and refrigeration equipment aboard ship. Inspect engines and other equipment. Stand engine-room watch, observing that lubricants and water levels are maintained in machinery and load on generators is within limits.

2nd – 3rd Engineer ($2,000-$3,000)
Certificate of Eligibility issued by accredited maritime school or facility. Excellent command of the English language. Knowledge and experience of modern marine plant ideally onboard of cruise liners. Good IT skills and ability to manipulate modern Windows based packages.

Engaged in watchkeeping duties on a rotational basis with other 2nd Engineers. Supervise lower rank engineers. Manage and control of main plant from Engine Control Room. Maintenance duties in and around the marine plant on a modern cruise liner including power generation, engine maintenance, oil purification, etc. Control and maintenance of passenger services equipment.

Chief Air-conditioning Engineer ($2,500-$3,000)
Graduation diploma from accredited maritime school. Extensive engineering experience onboard or equivalent on land.

Supervise all air-conditioning and refrigeration systems onboard. Inspect maintenance, operation, and repair work for compliance with the standards and the safety procedures.

Air-Conditioning Technician ($2,000-$2,500)
Preferred graduate at accredited maritime school. All necessary certificates and licenses. Experience in similar secondary position. All necessary certificates and licenses.

Boilerman ($1,000-$1,300)
Required professional experience or equivalent apprenticeship program/training.

Locate and mark reference points for columns or plates on foundation using master straightedge, square, transit and other measuring instruments. Inspect the ship for faulty accessories and pressure test for leakage. Maintain and repair stationary steam boilers and boiler house auxiliaries. Repair insulation of pressure vessel with cement.

Bolt or arc-welds pressure vessel structures and parts together.

Carpenter ($1,000-$1,300)
Required in-depth experience as a carpenter at sea or on land.

Shape irregular parts and trims excess material from bulkhead and furnishings to ensure fit meets specifications. Repair structural woodwork and replace defective parts and equipment. Assemble and install hardware, gaskets, furnishings, floors, or insulation. Transfer dimensions or measurements of wood parts or bulkhead on plywood. Cut wood or glass to specified dimensions.

Electrician ($1,500-$3,500)
Graduation diploma from accredited maritime school plus all applicable certificates and licenses. At least 2-4 years of experience in related position onboard.

Ensure maintenance of all electrical devises on board the vessel. Provide electrical support to the Engine Room Team. Repair and maintain electrical equipment such as generators, motors, alternators, and intercommunication systems aboard ship. Perform routine tests to ensure that electric motors are driving pumps, blowers, and refrigerating machinery. Test wiring for short circuits.

Electronic Engineer ($2,500-$3,500)
Associate degree in Electronics-Electrical technology. Onboard experience or equivalent.

In charge of all electronics and navigational equipment on the vessel. Test electronics unit using standard test equipment. Evaluate performance and determine needs for adjustments. Design basic circuitry and sketches for design documentation as directed by engineers using drafting instruments and computer aided design equipment.

Refrigeration Engineer ($2,000-$3,000)
At least 1-2 years onboard experience plus all applicable certificates and licenses.

Install and repair industrial and commercial refrigerating systems. Fabricate and assemble components and structural portions of refrigeration system. Adjust valves according to specifications and charges system with specified type of refrigerant. Observe system operation, using gauges and instruments, and adjusts or replaces mechanisms and parts, according to specifications.

Engine Repairman ($1,500-$2,500)
Required onboard experience or equivalent.

Maintain and repair all engines and diesel-fueled equipment.

Fire Fighter ($1,400-$2,000)
Associate degree or higher in Fire Science plus all necessary certificates such as a paramedical license.

Control and extinguish fires, protect life and property, and maintain equipment. Respond to fire alarms and other emergency calls. Select hose nozzle depending on type of fire, and direct stream of water or chemicals onto fire. Protect property from water and smoke.

Fitter ($1,400-$2,000)
Required extensive experience in a similar position preferably onboard.

Lay out reference points and dimensions on metal, plastic stock or workpieces such as sheets, tubes, castings, plates, structural shapes, or machine parts for further processing. Plan and develop layout from blueprints and templates applying knowledge of trigonometry, design, effects of heat, and properties of metal.

Machinist ($1,400-$2,000)
Required extensive experience in a similar position preferably onboard.

Operate assigned machines onboard. Maintain onboard equipment.

Mechanic ($1,400-$2,000)
Required extensive experience in a similar position preferably onboard.

Maintain and repair various onboard equipment and machines.

Motorman ($1,400-$2,000)
Related experience or apprenticeship program/training.

Operate various machines and equipment. Maintain and clean assigned engines.

Oilier ($1,400-$2,000)
Related experience or apprenticeship program/training.

Oil and grease moving parts such as gears, shafts, and bearings of engines and auxiliary equipment used to propel maritime vessels. Read pressure and temperature gauges. Record data in engineering log. Examine machinery for specified pressure and flow of lubricants. Fill oil cups on machinery according to machinery lubrication instructions.

Plumber ($2,000-$2,400)
Graduation diploma from accredited maritime school. At least 1-2 years onboard experience.

Repair and maintain plumbing by replacing defective washers, replacing or mending broken pipes, and opening clogged drains. Assemble pipe sections, tubing and fittings using screws, bolts, etc. Cut opening in structures to accommodate pipes and pipe fittings.

Locate and mark position of pipe installations and passage holes in structures.

Upholsterer ($1,500-$2,000)
Related experience or apprenticeship program/training.

Make, repair, or replace upholstery onboard. Repair frame of work piece. Measure and cut new covering material. Stack, align, and smooth material on cutting table. Examine upholstery to locate defects. Draw cutting lines on material following pattern, templates, sketches, or blueprints.

Wiper ($1,000-$1,800)
Related experience or apprenticeship program/training.

Maintain cleanliness of engines and engineers' workshops and offices.

Entertainment Department

Cruise Director ($3,000-$4,800)
2+ years experience on cruise ship preferably starting from entertainment entry level position. Willingness to be all the time at the spotlight. Excellent public speaking and organizational skills. Provide the guests with onboard and shore activities by directing the development and implementation of ship and shore programs in accordance with the high quality of Company's product and services to the guests. May arrange transportation, activity equipment, and services of medical personnel.

Assistant Cruise Director ($2,000-$3,200)
2+ years experience on cruise ship preferably starting from entertainment entry level position. Excellent public speaking and organizational skills. Very energetic and flexible personality. Able to communicate and deal with many types of people.

Oversee the entire department and cruise staff. Arrange all necessary supplies for the productions. Schedule and assign tasks to the cruise staff. Make sure all the time that everything is running smoothly.

Cruise Consultant ($2,000-$2,300)
Experience in sales and marketing, cruise bookings or customer relations.

Generate future cruise bookings through events, appointments, public functions and consultations. Hold desk hours. Socialize with the passengers to promote future cruises.

Social Host/ess ($1,500-$3,000)
Outgoing, friendly and helpful personality. Excellent communication and public speaking skills. Knowledge of good etiquette is a plus.

Welcome guests, seat them at tables or in lounge, and help ensure quality of facilities and service. Arrange parties or special service for diners. Inspect dining room serving stations for neatness and cleanliness. Requisition linens and other supplies for tables and serving stations. Adjust complaints of guests.

Cruise Staff ($1,200-$2,400)
Very outgoing, dynamic and guests oriented personality. Excellent communication skills and high endurance to fulfill numerous different tasks every day.

Participate in various entertainment and pool activities. Answer any questions. Participate in the weekly drills. May assist guests with their luggage upon embarkation-disembarkation.

Cruise Staff Steward ($1,000-$2,000)
Entry level position. Previous experience in Banquet or Housekeeping will be a plus.

Assist with set up and tear down of stage decors and equipment.

Clean assigned stage areas. There are excellent promotional opportunities.

Disc Jockey ($1,200-$2,000)
Experience as DJ and in-depth knowledge of the latest hits. Very outgoing and dynamic personality. Able to manipulate comprehensive audio and video equipment. Provide great experience for the guests in the disco.

Youth Coordinator ($1,600-$2,800)
Experience as youth coordinator. Summer camp youth counselor, certified teacher or student with major in Child education/psychology. Excellent organizational skills, dynamic and creative attitude backed with strong interest in working with many children.

Take active participation in the numerous activities for children. Make sure that all children are involved and enjoy their time. May perform duties as cruise staff if necessary.

The 11 cruise lines, which currently have youth programs are: Royal Caribbean, Princess, Carnival, Celebrity, Cunard, Disney, Norwegian, Holland America, Windjammer, Festival and Costa cruises.

Sound & Light Technician ($1,200-$2,000)
Support the audio and video system in all aspects on board. Operate machines and equipment to record, synchronize, mix, or reproduce music, voices and sound effects in sporting arenas, theater productions or video productions. Set up, adjust, and test recording equipment to prepare for recording session. Record speech, music, and other sounds on recording media using recording equipment.

TV Station Manager ($1,200-$3,000)
BA in Communications with major preferably in television production or related experience. In-depth knowledge of camera operation, production and editing. Knowledge of maintenance of

the equipment a plus.

Plan and direct audio and video aspects of television programs, based on program specifications and knowledge of television programming techniques. Interpret script, rehearse cast, and establish pace of program to stay within time requirements. Inform technicians of scenery, lights, props, and other equipment desired.

Stage Manager ($2,000-$2,500)
Associate degree in AV programming or few years experience.

Interpret script, conduct rehearsals, and direct activities of cast and technical crew for stage. Establish pace of program and sequences of scenes according to time requirements, cast and set accessibility. Direct cast, crew, and technicians during production.

AV Coordinator ($1,500-$2,000)
1+ years professional experience.

Install rigging, lighting, sound equipment, and scenery. Erect stages for theatrical, musical, and other entertainment events. Read stage layout specifications, blueprints. Confer with Stage Manager to determine type and location of props, sets, lighting, scenery, and sound equipment required for specific event.

AV Technician/Operator ($1,200-$2,000)
1+ years professional experience. Support all aspects of the audio and video system onboard. Direct and coordinate activities of assistants and other personnel during production. Develop production ideas based on assignment or generate own ideas based on objectives and interest. Set up, adjust, and operate equipment such as cameras, recorders, and sound mixers during production. Determine approach, format, level, content, and medium to meet objectives most effectively within budgetary constraints.

Guest Entertainer ($3,000-$6,000)

Professional experience or training as magician, dancer, musician, singer, ventriloquist, comedian or juggler. Send a video portfolio to the agencies hiring for the cruise lines.

Work up to 10 hours per week as the guest star in stage productions. Usually go from one cruise line's ship to another.

Singer ($1,600-$4,000)
Required professional experience. Include an audio/video portfolio in your application.

Memorize musical selections or sing following printed text, musical notation, or guest requests. Sing a cappella or with musical accompaniment before audience as soloist, in group, or as member of vocal ensemble. Interpret or modify music to individualize presentation and maintain audience interest. Practice songs and routine to maintain and improve vocal skills.

Dance Instructor ($1,200-$2,400)
Required professional experience and pass of audition. Send your portfolio on a video tape.

Perform up to 10 hours per week as cruise staff. Take part in several shows per week.

Dancer ($1,200-$3,000)
Required professional experience and passing of audition.

Perform classical, modern, or acrobatic dances in productions. May coordinate dancing with that of partner or dance ensemble. Rehearse solo, with partners or troupe members. Work with choreographer to refine or modify dance steps. Study and practice dance moves required in role. Audition for parts in production.

Musician ($1,400-$2,000)
Required professional experience as instrumentalist.

Play musical instrument as soloist or as ember of musical group. May memorize musical scores. Study and rehearse music to learn and interpret score. Practice performance on musical instrument to maintain and improve skills. Transpose music to play in alternate key or fit in individual style.

Band Musician ($1,200-$2,400)
Required professional experience and ability to play several styles of music. Send an audio/video portfolio. Groups should have complete set.

Play during parties, celebrations and at show productions. The larger cruise lines need groups performing different music styles.

Band Leader ($1,600-$2,400)
Required professional experience as a musical director and knowledge of musical charts.

Direct musicians during performances and shows.

Concessionaires

Salon Manager ($1,500-$3,200)
Previous experience at a management position or graduation diploma.

Manage business operations and direct personal service functions of beauty salon. Confer with employees to ensure quality services for guests such as hair styling, facials, manicures and massages. Adjust customer complaints and promote new business by expressing personal interest in efficient service for guests. Keep accounts of receipts and expenditures and make up payroll. Order equipment and supplies.

Beauty Therapist ($1,200-$2,000)

Licensed professional with 1+ years of experience.

Provide beauty services for customers. Suggest cosmetics for conditions such as dry or oily skin. Apply creams and lotions to customer's face and neck to soften skin and lubricate tissues.

Manicurist ($1,200-$2,000)
2+ years of professional experience.

Clean and shape customers' fingernails and toenails. Apply clear or colored liquid polish onto nails with brush. Remove paper forms or shapes and smooth edges of nails. Remove previously applied nail polish. Brush coats of powder and solvent onto nails and paper forms with hand brush to maintain nail appearance and to extend nails to desired length. Polish nails, using powdered polishes and buffer.

Hairstylist ($1,200-$2,400)
Certified professional with 2+ years of experience.

Analyze hair to ascertain its condition. Cut, trim and shape hair using clippers, scissors, trimmers and razors. Massage and treat scalp using hands and fingers. Bleach, die, or tint hair using applicator or brush. Administer therapeutic medication or advise guests to seek medical treatment for chronic or contagious scalp conditions. Comb, brush, and spray hair or wigs to set style.

Massage Therapist ($1,200-$2,400)
Certified professional with 1+ years professional experience.

Massage customers and administer other body conditioning treatments for hygienic or remedial purposes. Massage body using different techniques to stimulate blood circulation, relax contracted muscles, facilitate elimination of waste matter, or relieve other conditions. May administer steam, dry heat, or water treatments on request. Give directions to clients for activities such as reducing weight or remedial exercises.

Spa Attendant ($800-$1,400)
Previous experience in Spa or Recreation. CPR certificate a plus.

Provide supplies to the guests such as towels and soap. Collect soiled linen, mop assigned dressing room, wash shower room walls and clean bathroom facilities.

Sports Director ($1,500-$2,000)
Previous experience in coordinating sports activities in hotel/resort. Previous management position is a plus. Certified in CPR and First Aid. Excellent communication and organizational skills.

Supervise the sports activities onboard. Organize and plan games, tournaments and recreation activities. Direct the guests towards appropriate sport activities.

Fitness/Aerobics Instructor ($1,200-$2,400)
Certified instructor plus CPR and First aid. In-depth knowledge of fitness programs and equipment.

Teach individual and team sports to participants. Show proper techniques and recommend exercises according to the guests' physical capabilities. Teach and demonstrate use of gymnastic and training apparatus such as trampolines and weights. Explain and enforce safety rules and regulations. Organize, lead, instruct, and referee indoor and outdoor games. Plan physical education programs to promote development of guests' physical capabilities and social skills.

Water Sports Instructor ($1,700-$2,000)
Experience as scuba and snorkeling instructor. Membership in PADI, NAUI or SSI. Certified in First Aid and CPR plus additional water sports like parasailing.

Teach snorkeling and diving during shore excursions. Give also classes for the guests onboard. Maintain the equipment in excellent condition.

Internet Instructor ($1,500-$2,000)
Previous experience and diploma in IT/Computer Science preferred. Excellent customer relations, problem solving and troubleshooting.

Provide guests with professional, courteous and high quality training and services for computer and Internet use.

Gift Shop Manager ($1,600-$3,200)
Previous retail management position or onboard experience.

Coordinate sales promotions and prepare merchandise display and advertising copy. Formulate pricing policies on merchandise according to requirements for profitability of store operations. Examine merchandise to ensure that it is correctly priced, displayed or functions as advertised. Prepare sales and inventory reports for management and budget departments.

Gift Shop Assistant ($1,200-$2,400)
Retails experience preferably in selling jewelry, watches, clothes, cosmetics, gifts, etc. or public relations background.

Assist customers in trying on merchandise. Clean shelves, counters, and tables. Requisition new stock. Wrap merchandise. Maintain records related to sales. Recommend, select, and obtain merchandise based on customer needs and desires. Total purchases, receive payment, make change, or process credit transaction.

Casino Manager ($2,800-$3,600)
Graduation diploma from casino school. At least 3 years experience in a management position within the casino industry.

Direct dealers compiling summary sheets for each race or event to show amount wagered and amount to be paid to winners. Establish policies on types of gambling offered, extension of credit, odds, and serving food and beverages. Explain and interpret house rules such as game rules and betting limits to guests.

Assistant Casino Manager ($1,500-$2,000)
At least 3 years experience within the casino industry. In-depth knowledge of all casino games.

Supervise the day to day operation. Address and resolve any customer concerns or questions.

Croupier/Dealer ($1,200-$2,400)
2+ years experience in the gambling industry or diploma from a casino school with at least 2 games- poker, roulette, craps and blackjack.

Conduct gambling table or game such as dice, roulette, cards, or keno and ensure that game rules are followed. Assist operators or customers in conducting games of chance. Participate in game for gambling establishment to provide minimum complement of players at table. Verify, compute, and pay out winnings.

Slot Technician ($1,600-$2,400)
2+ years experience in maintaining and repairing slot machines.

Collect coins from machines and make settlements with concessionaires. Disassemble and assemble machines. Test dispensing, electrical, coin-handling, carbonation, refrigeration, or ice-making machines. Adjust and repair vending machines and meters. Replace defective electrical and mechanical parts.

Casino Cashier ($1,000-$2,000)
Preferred is previous experience at such position. Excellent money handling skills.

Accept and pay off bets placed by guests in cardrooms, bookmaking or other gambling establishments. Accept cash or checks for chips or approve guests' credit and charge individual accounts for amount issued. Accept credit applications and verify credit references to obtain check-cashing authorization.

Photo Shop Manager ($1,600-$3,200)
Required 2+ years at a management position or previous experience as a photographer preferably onboard. Direct activities of photographers assisting in setting up the equipment. College degree is a serious advantage. Responsible for the entire operation of the Photo Shop. Supervise the fast and defect-free development of the films.

Photographer ($1,400-$2,400)
Preferred is professional experience or a diploma. Knowledge of developing films is a plus. Portfolio with creative or professional photographic work will make you to stand out.

Arrange subject material in desired position. Frame subject matter and background in lens to capture desired image. Focus camera and adjust settings based on lighting, distance, subject material and film speed. Estimate or measure light level, distance, and number of exposure needed.

Shore Excursions Manager ($2,400-$3,600)
College education is preferred. Previous travel related job-experience. In-depth knowledge of all ports of calls. Fluent English and 1+ other languages. Proficiency in Word, Excel and Fidelio.

Plan tour itinerary. Apply knowledge of travel routes and destination sites. Explain applicable laws to the groups to ensure compliance. Verify quantity and quality of equipment or supplies to ensure prerequisite needs for tours have been met. Select activity tour sites, lead groups to selected locations and describe points of interest.

Asst. Excursions Manager ($1,600-$2,400)
High School degree or higher. Previous experience in the travel industry. Fluent English and 1+ other languages. Proficiency in Word, Excel and Fidelio.

Provide guests with port information. Assist Non-English speaking guests in all matters. Dispatch of tour buses and private cars. Escort tours and assign tour escorts. Coordinate with F&B Department various requirements for tours: water, lunch boxes. Man tour desk, sale issuing of tickets. Prepare end of day reports for tour sales programs.

Shore Excursions Staff ($1,600-$2,400)
Excellent communication and organizational skills.

Perform clerical duties such as typing, filing, operating switchboard, and delivering of mail and messages. Escort group on port tours, describe points of interest and respond to questions. Distribute brochures and convey background information. Explain processes and operations at tour site.

Port Lecturer ($2,000-$3,500)
Experienced professional from the travel industry with in-depth knowledge of the ports of call. Public relations or sales and marketing background is a definite plus.

Art Auctioneer ($2,000-$3,500)
In-depth experience in sales, art actions and public speaking.

Medical Department

Doctor/Physician ($4,000-$8,000)
At least 3 years post graduate experience with particular emphasis in A&E or acute medicine such as ICU/CCU. Current US or UK board certification. Possession of a valid accredited ALS/ACLS certificate

prior to joining a ship.

Deal with the overall management of the Medical Department and the treatment of the passengers. Required to conduct morning and evening consultations for the crew and be on call at night for emergency visits or admissions.

Nurse ($2,400-$4,000)
At least 3 years post registration experience with particular emphasis in A&E or acute medicine such as ICU/CCU. Current US or UK nurse license with appropriate Governmental regulatory body. Possession of a valid accredited ALS/ACLS certificate prior to joining a ship.

Assist the Medical Officer(s) in the overall management of the Department and treatment of the patients. Assist in the smooth running of morning and evening consultations for the crew and passengers. Be on call for emergency visits or admissions. Provide routine and emergency nursing care for all passengers and crew.

Hotel Department

Hotel Manager ($4,000-$4,800)
Bachelor's degree in Hospitality Management, Business Administration or related field. 5+ years experience as General Manager, Resident Manager, or Director of Operations in hotel or cruise ship (high volume preferred). Fluent English preferably with 1+ additional languages.

Oversees the entire Hotel department. Observe and monitor performance to ensure efficient operations and adherence to the policies and procedures. Plan, direct, and coordinate activities within the department. Serve as a coordinator the hotel and the other departments. Assign duties to staff and schedules shifts. Approve purchases of supplies and arrange any necessary outside services.

Assistant Hotel Manager ($2,500-$3,500)

Degree in Hotel Management. Minimum 2+ years experience within a hotel or cruise ship. Computer knowledge: Word, Excel, and Fidelio. Familiar with in-house hotel systems including night audit function. Effective communication skills both written and oral. Able to meet deadlines, plans and prioritize workloads. Effective complaint handling and Guest Relations skills.

Desktop Publisher ($1,200-$2,000)
Excellent knowledge of graphical user interface: Word, PageMaker and Corel Draw. Knowledge of the following peripherals: scanner, CD/R drive and high resolution laser printer. Excellent command of English and preferably 1 additional language.

Coordinate the entire desktop publishing onboard. Read and answer correspondence. File and retrieve documents, records and reports. Coordinate and direct office services, records and budget preparation to aid executives. Prepare records and reports such as recommendations for solutions of administrative problems and annual reports. Responsible for all onboard printed matters and timely production.

Accountant/Auditor ($1,500-$2,000)
Degree in Accounting, Finance or similar major. Preferred is additional Associate degree in Hotel and Restaurant Management or hotel experience.

Prepare balance sheet, profit and loss statement, amortization and depreciation schedules as well as other financial reports. Analyze records of financial transactions to determine accuracy and completeness of entries. Report finances to management and advise about resource utilization, tax strategies, and assumptions underlying budget forecasts. Develop, maintain, analyze budgets, and prepare periodic reports comparing budgeted costs to actual costs. Audit contracts, and prepare reports to substantiate transactions prior to settlement.

Chief Purser ($2,800-$3,600)
Required Hotel Administration or financial background. Previous ship experience in Administration/Accounting, Cashier, Crew Purser, or First Purser. Fluent English and preferably 1 additional language. Proficiency in Word, Excel, PowerPoint and Fidelio.

Ensure smooth and accurate onboard financial operation. Coordinate the payroll for onboard employees. Facilitate prompt processing of legal documents with port authorities by preparing required paper work. Provide guests with promptly, friendly, efficient service by directing the Reception Desk operation and administrative functions of the ship. Ensure guests and crew clearance procedures are followed through, and serve as contact with the Port's agents.

1st Purser ($2,400-$3,200)
Coordinate activities of staff aboard ship concerned with shipboard business functions and social activities for passengers. Maintain payroll records and pay off crews at completion of voyage. Assist passengers in preparing declarations for customs, arranging for inspections of horticultural items being brought into country and inspection of documents by immigration authorities. Provide banking services and safekeeping of valuables for passengers. Prepare shipping articles and signs on crew.

2nd - 3rd Purser ($2,000-$3,200)
2+ years previous Front Office experience. Work well under pressure. Punctual, courteous and reliable. Knowledge of customs regulations and laws. Supervision of the receptionists. Check in and check out of the guests. Ability to deal with a large amount of money. Deal with reports, forms and guest requests.

Crew Purser/Assistant ($1,000-$2,000)
Provide administrative support for the ship and crew by processing crew paperwork and assist with all crew-related matters. Assign ID card to the crew. Arrange all necessary supplies for the staff. Liaison between the Officers and the crew.

Systems Manager ($5,000-$7,000)
Required 4+ years of related experience plus degree in Computer Science or Information Technology. Proven IT management knowledge and experience. Excellent troubleshooting and communicational skills.

In charge of all communication devices on board the vessel. Direct training of subordinates. Approve, prepare, monitor, and adjust operational budget. Consult with users, management, vendors, and technicians to determine computing needs and system requirements. Direct daily operations of department and coordinate project activities with other departments. Evaluate data processing project proposals and assess project feasibility.

Receptionist ($1,000-$2,000)
Preferably 2+ years experience as receptionist, Hotel School degree and accounting knowledge. Fluent in English and in 1+ additional languages. Proficiency in Word, Excel, Outlook and Fidelio.

Answer telephone to schedule future appointments. Provide information or forward calls. Type memos, correspondence, travel vouchers and other documents.

Record, compile, enter, and retrieve information. Hear and resolve complaints from guests. Receive payment and record receipts for services. Monitor facility to ensure compliance with regulations.

F&B Department

F&B Manager ($2,800-$3,500)
Degree in Hospitality Management and applicable food handling certificates. 3+ years F&B experience preferably on a cruise ship.

Fluent English and additional language is welcomed. Proficiency in Word, Excel and Fidelio.

Coordinate assignments of cooking personnel to ensure economical use of food and timely preparation. Test cooked food to ensure palatability and flavor conformity. Review menus, analyze recipes to determine labor and overhead costs, and assign prices to menu items. Monitor budget, payroll records, and review financial transactions to ensure expenditures are authorized and budgeted. Estimate food, liquor, wine, and other beverage consumption to anticipate amount to be purchased or requisitioned.

Asst. F&B Manager ($2,400-$3,000)
Degree in Hospitality Management preferred as well as applicable food handling certificates. 2+ years F&B experience preferably on a cruise ship. Good management skills.

Purchase or requisition supplies and equipment to ensure quality and timely delivery of services. Recommend measures to improve work procedures and staff performance to increase quality of services and job safety. Supervise and coordinate preparing and serving of food and other related duties. Collaborate with specified personnel to plan menus, serving arrangements, and related details. Receive, issue, take inventory of supplies and equipment, and report shortages to designated personnel.

F&B Accountant/Controler ($2,000-$2,600)
Good product knowledge of meat, fish and fresh products as well as beverages. Well-organized with strong leadership skills.

Manage all ordering and issuing for the Hotel department. Make inventory and cost control of hotel stores. Coordinate all orders for food, beverages, sundries and consumables. Receiving, storage and internal distribution of hotel stores.

Dinning Room Manager ($2,000-$4,000)
Preferred is degree in Hospitality Management. Strong F&B or Culinary background and management skills. Excellent knowledge

of food, beverage and international cuisine. Fluent English and preferably 1+ additional languages.

Provide guests with quality food and beverage service by managing the dining room and overseeing the operations of the bars. Ensure smooth running of restaurant and bar areas. Inspect dining room serving stations for neatness and cleanliness. Assign work tasks and coordinate activities of the personnel to ensure prompt and courteous service. Implement and maintain guidelines, procedures and training practices set by the corporate office. Requisition table linens and other supplies for tables and serving stations.

Assistant Maitre d' ($2,000-$3,200)
2+ years at a management position in hotel or ship. Strong Culinary/F&B background with all applicable certificates. Fluent English and preferably 1 additional language. Supervise day to day operation of a restaurant. Inspect cleanliness and proper set up. Enforce compliance with the highest standards of food preparation and serving.

Head Waiter ($2,000-$3,800)
Diploma from accredited college. 1+ years F&B experience preferably on a cruise ship. Excellent knowledge of international cuisine and table side service. Fluent English and 1+ additional languages.

Provide guests with professional food and beverage service by supervising the wait staff in the dining room(s). Produce working routines for the restaurant that will provide adequate staff levels. Good knowledge of catering practices.

Maintain prescribed systems for the monitoring and control of stock and relevant costs in accordance with company procedures. Responsible for special orders and solving guest complaints.

Dinning Room Waiter ($2,400-$3,600)
Diploma from a recognized apprenticeship program, or equivalent.

1+ years F&B related experience preferably on a cruise ship.

Excellent knowledge of international cuisine. Fluent English and preferably 1+ additional languages.

Present menu to guests, suggest food or beverage selections, and answer questions regarding preparation and service. Take orders for food or beverage. Serve meals or beverages to guests. Compute cost of meal or beverage. Accept payment and return change, or refer guests to Cashier. Remove dishes and glasses from table or counter and take them to kitchen for cleaning.

Busboy ($1,000-$1,500)
Prepare sandwiches, salads, and other short-order items. Replenish foods at serving stations. Accept payment for food, using cash register or adding machine to total check. Call order to kitchen, pick up and serve order when it is ready. Serve food, beverages, or desserts to customers in variety of settings such as take out counter of restaurant or lunchroom.

Snack-Buffet Steward ($1,000-$1,400)
Entry level position.

Brew coffee and tea and fills containers with requested beverages. Carve meat. Scrub and polish counters, steamtables, and other equipment. Clean glasses and dishes. Wrap menu items such as sandwiches, hot entrees, and desserts. Add relishes and garnishes according to instructions.

Bar Manager ($2,000-$3,200)
At least 2 years bar experience. Excellent knowledge of preparation, garnishing and glassware for all beverages served according to Company's standards. Knowledge of cocktail lists, champagne bar and wine menu. Fluent English.

Provide high quality service to guests by directing the operation of all beverage operations. Estimate and order bar stuffs, liquors, wines and other beverages and supplies. Plan menus, serving arrangements, and other related details. Ensure efficient and smooth beverage operation according to Company's standards. Comply with all legal, safety, hygiene and administration procedures. Maximize revenue and profit margins in assigned outlet(s).

Bartender ($1,600-$3,200)
1-2 years bartender experience. Excellent knowledge of bar service. Fluent English and preferably 1+ additional languages.

Mix ingredients such as liquor, water, soda, sugar, and bitters to prepare cocktails and other drinks. May prepare appetizers such as pickles, cheese, and cold meats. Slice and pit fruit for garnishing drinks. Clean glasses, utensils, and bar equipment. Order or requisition liquors and supplies. Arrange bottles and glasses to make attractive display.

Assistant Bartender ($1,000-$1,500)
Experience in a hotel, club or restaurant. Thorough knowledge of wines and liquors.

Ensure smooth and efficient operation of the bar under the direction of the Bartender to achieve guest satisfaction. Serve shots (jiggers) for consumption. Serve bottled beer or draw draught beer from kegs. Sell unopened bottles of alcoholic and nonalcoholic beverages to be taken from premises when licensed for sale of packaged goods. Receive payment for amount of sale and make change. Contribute to the creation and maintenance of an enthusiastic, motivated working environment.

Cocktail Wait Staff ($1,600-$2,400)
Entry level job. Previous F&B experience is a plus.

Prepare and serve cocktails. Pour champagne and other drinks at cocktail parties. Provide courteous and professional beverage service.

Chief Wine Steward ($1,600-$3,000)
At least 3 years Sommelier experience. Excellent wine and bar knowledge. Preferred are cruise ship experience, fluent English and basic French pronunciation.

Organization and supervision of all aspects of beverage service onboard. Provide guests with courteous, professional champagne and wine service. Organize wine tastings for guests. Monitor and control beverage costs. Responsible for the onboard Wine Selection.

Wine Steward ($1,400-$2,8000)
Sommelier diploma and/or certificates from specialized courses, programs, or seminars. At least 2 years experience as a Sommelier in 4/5 star establishments. Strong command of the English language. A good knowledge of the products and regions represented by Company's wine program.

Provide guests with courteous, professional champagne and wine service. Manage a station in the dining room by providing great wine service and taking advantage of all opportunities to increase beverage sales. Conduct Wine Seminars and Castings for the guests. Provide Wine Training Sessions for Restaurant and Bar staff. Pair wines with food recommending those that will complement the different styles of cuisine and the different methods of food preparation.

Housekeeping Department

Executive Housekeeper ($2,500-$3,500)
3+ years of management experience in a hotel or cruise ship. Fluent English and preferably 1+ additional languages. Computer knowledge, strong leadership skills and practice "leadership by example".

Supervision of the entire Housekeeping department. Maintain highest standards of cleanliness in guest suites and public areas as well as in Officer and Crew areas. Responsible for supervision of laundry and flower shop. Direct all housekeeping program to ensure clean, orderly, and attractive conditions onboard. Establish standards and procedures for work of housekeeping staff, and plan work schedules to ensure adequate service.

Asst. Executive Housekeeper ($2,000-$2,500)
2+ years of management experience in a hotel or cruise ship.

In charge of the day to day operation of the department. Supervise the cleanliness of the passenger cabins. In charge of scheduling, inventory, and requisition. Supervise handling of passenger luggage at the beginning and at the end of the cruise.

Head Steward ($1,200-$2,400)
2+ years housekeeping experience in a hotel or cruise ship. Management experience preferred.

Prepare assignments for staff and inspect the cleanliness. Investigate complaints regarding housekeeping service and equipment, and take corrective action. Conduct orientation and in-service training. Explain policies, work procedures, and demonstrate proper use and maintenance of equipment. Determine need for repairs or replacement of furniture and make recommendations. Attend staff meetings to discuss company policies and guests' complaints. Prepare reports concerning room occupancy, payroll, and department expenses.

Cabin Steward/ess ($1,200-$2,400)
Previous housekeeping experience. Fluent English and preferably 1+ additional languages. Pleasant, positive and energetic personality.

Clean rooms, hallways, lobbies, lounges, restrooms, corridors, elevators, stairways, lockers and other assigned areas. Polish metalwork such as fixtures and fittings. Move and arrange furniture, turn mattresses, hang draperies, dust venetian blinds, and prepare hotel facilities for occupancy. Deliver ironing boards, baby cribs, and rollaway beds to guests' rooms. Wash windows, sills, and door panels. Collect soiled linens for laundering, and receive and store linen supplies in linen closet.

Deck Steward ($1,000-$1,600)
Clean and polish wood trim, brass, and other metal parts. Chip and clean rust spots on deck, superstructure, and sides of ship using wire brush and hand or air-chipping machine. Sweep and wash deck using broom, mops, brushes, and hose. Handle lines to moor vessel to wharf, tie up vessel to another vessel, or rig towing lines. Examine machinery for specified pressure and flow of lubricants. Read pressure and temperature displays, and record data in engineering log.

Chief Linen Keeper ($1,200-$2,000)
Supervise and coordinate activities of staff engaged in laundering linens and wearing apparel. Assign duties to staff. Inventory articles in stock such as table linens, towels, bed sheets, and uniforms. Confer with superintendent to request replacement of articles in short supply. Count articles to ensure agreement with quantity specified on load sheet. Resolve customer complaints and modify orders according to size, color, and type of articles specified.

Bell Captain ($1,200-$2,000)
Previous hotel or cruise ship experience preferably at a supervisory position.

Supervise Bellmen engaged in duties such as paging, running errands, and giving information. Inspect staff for neatness and uniform dress. Instruct staff in procedures regarding requests from guests, utilizing knowledge of hotel facilities and local merchants and attractions. Determine work schedules and keep time records. May perform duties of subordinates.

Bellman ($1,000-$1,600)

Previous hotel or cruise ship experience. Polite and outgoing personality.

Escort incoming guests to rooms, assist with hand luggage, and offer information pertaining to available services and facilities, points of interest, and entertainment attractions. Explain features of room such as operation of radio, television, night-lock, and how to place telephone calls.

May deliver room service orders. Pick up articles for laundry and valet service. Escort guests in lobby, dining room, or other places onboard. Deliver messages and run errands.

Culinary Department

Executive Chef ($2,400-$4,000)
Coordinate activities, direct indoctrination and training of chefs, cooks, and other kitchen staff. Plan or participate in planning of menus and utilization of food surpluses and leftovers, taking into account marketing conditions, probable number of guests, popularity of various dishes, and recency of menu. Estimate food consumption and purchase or requisition foodstuffs and kitchen supplies. Maintain time and payroll records. Review menus, analyze recipes, determine food, labor, and overhead costs. Assign prices to menu items.

Assistant Executive Chef ($1,600-$2,800)
5+ years Chef de Cuisine experience in a 5 star operation: hotel, restaurant or ship. Excellent knowledge of food, beverage and international cuisine. Computer knowledge: Word, Excel, AmiPro and Fidelio. Fluent English and preferably additional 1+ languages.

Ensure smooth running operation of department. Supervision and daily schedule planning for galley crew. Daily lunch and dinner menu briefing with galley crew, head waiters and dining room staff. Estimate amounts and costs, and requisition supplies and equipment to ensure efficient operation. Check and supervise service hours (breakfast, lunch and dinner), announce orders, check arranged plates and ensure immediate service. Collaborate with specified personnel. Plan and develop recipes and menus.

Chef de Partie ($2,000-$2,500)
Chefs diploma from a recognized institution. 2+ years experience in 4/5 star hotels or good quality volume catering operations. A Basic Food Hygiene Certificate and onboard experience is preferred.

Provide the guests with the highest quality product by organizing and preparing food at assigned stations. Participate in daily menu briefing with Sous Chef and Executive Chef. Prepare and present dishes in accordance with the corporate menu cycles. Coordinate and supervise Assistant Cooks. Order special products to Baker and/or other First Cooks. Ensure all cooks report to duty on time. Ensure smooth and efficient operation of allocated sections such as crew galley, soup section or vegetable section.

Souse Chef ($2,500-$3,500)
4+ years in a similar secondary position. An Advanced Food Hygiene Certificate is desirable. Fluent English and proficiency in Word and AmiPro. Knowledge of U.S.P.H. standards and procedures a plus.

Ensure smooth and efficient operation of allocated F&B outlets. Assist Executive Chef with menu planning. Participate in daily menu briefing of lunch and dinner with galley crew. Assist in guest chef programs, special functions, galley tours and cooking demos. Supervise the operation and delivery of the Corporate menu cycles. Maintain exceptionally high hygiene standards in accordance with the Company Food Safety Policy.

General Cook ($1,200-$2,000)
2+ years hotel, restaurant or cruise ship experience

Preparation of food in accordance with the highest Company's standards.

Executive Pastry Chef ($2,500-$3,500)
5 years pastry experience, 1 year Pastry Chef experience with 5 star operation: hotel, restaurant or ship. Fluent English asnd preferably additional 1+ languages. Ability to perform under pressure.

Production of all pastries for lunch, teatime and dinner. Supervision and briefing of pastry team. Ensure all bread for lunch and dinner is served warm and on time. Check special orders, functions and cocktail parties. Assign specific baking tasks and direct staff in task performance. Ensure food items returned to galley are distributed and stored properly. Requisitioning of all necessary products for pastry shop.

Pastry Chef ($1,500-$2,500)
2+ years experience in 5 star operation: hotel, restaurant or ship. Able to work independently. Ability to perform well under pressure. Innovative and punctual.

Provide guests with the highest quality desserts and baked goods. Produce puddings, icings, and fancy pastries. Decorate products with icing designs using spatula and cream bag. Create new designs and recipes. Requisition supplies and equipment. Knead doughs into desired shapes and place them in oven.

Crew Cook ($1,800-$2,400)
Graduation diploma preferred. Previous hotel, restaurant or cruise ship experience. Well-organized and punctual with good command of English.

Provide ship's Officers and Crew with variety and quality food. Coordination of Crew menus with Executive Chef. In charge of food service and handling. Requisition and checking of received items. In charge of crew galley and food counters. Ensure proper use of leftovers from main galley. Make general cleaning and maintenance according to specified standards. Assist management with training

and induction of new personnel.
Baker ($1,200-$2,500)

Previous culinary hotel, restaurant or cruise ship experience and diploma preferred. Independent, innovative and punctual.

Provide guests with the highest quality baked goods. Requisition all products for bakery. Mix and cook pie and pour fillings into pie shells and top them with meringue or cream. Mix ingredients to make icings, decorate cakes and pastries, and blend colors for icings, shaped ornaments, and statuaries. Cut, peel, and prepare fruit for pie fillings. Mold doughs in desired shapes or place them in greased or floured pans.

Butcher ($1,200-$2,000)
Previous culinary experience in a hotel, restaurant or cruise ship. Independent and punctual.

Responsible for all meat and fish for guests and crew. Correct storage of all butchery and defrosting procedures. Responsible for workstation, including meat and fish freezers in provision areas. Estimate requirements and requisition or order meat supply. Cut, trim, bone, tie, and grind meats such as beef, pork, poultry, and fish to prepare meat in cooking form. Receive, inspect, and store meat upon delivery.

Appendix D:
Complete Directory
Of All 73 Concessionaires' Addresses

Below are the agencies, recruiting firms and concessionaires, which are hiring for several types of cruise ship jobs. You have their names, complete addresses, telephones, faxes, and web sites. Use all this information to gather maximum details about a particular job and concessionaire. You will need them to write outstanding cover letter and resume.

Art Auctioneers

The PPI Group
4517 NW 31 Ave., Ft. Lauderdale
FL 33309, USA
Tel:+1 954 377-7777 Fax:+1 954 377-7000
www.ppigroup.com

Park West Galleries
29469 Northwestern Hwy
Southfield, MI 48034, USA
www.parkwestgallery.com

Beauty Salon and Spa

Canyon Ranch at Sea
Canyon Health Resorts, 8600 E. Rockcliff Road Tucson, AZ 85750, USA
Tel: +1 520 749-9000 Fax:+1 520-749-7759
www.canyonranchjobs.com

Mandara Spa Cruise Ship Div.
8125 NW 53rd Str., Suite 116
Miami, FL 33166, USA
Tel:+1 305 471-9553 Fax:+1 305 471-9501
www.mandaraspa.com

Steiner Leisure
770 South Dixie Highway, Suite 200
Coral Gables, FL 33146, USA
Tel:+1 305 358-9002 Fax:+1 305 372-9310
www.steinerleisure.com

Steiner Leisure Training Ltd.
The Lodge, 92 Uxbridge Road
Harrow Weald, Middix HA3 6BZ, UK
Tel :+44 208-909-5074 Fax:+44 208-909-5040
www.steinerleisure.com

Steiners of London- Canada
3539 Boul St. Charles, Suite 218
Kirkland, QC H9H 3C4, Canada
www.steinerleisure.com

Steiners of London- Australia
P.O. Box 2099, Camberwell West
Victoria 3124, Australia
www.steinerleisure.com

Steiners of London- Africa
Postnet Suite #270, Private Bag X 19,
Milnerton 7435, Cape Town, South Africa
www.steinerleisure.com

The Stylists Inc.
4644 Kolohala Str., Honolulu, HI 96816, USA
Tel:+1 808 923-3855 Fax: +1 808 736-6717

Harding Brothers
Avonmouth Way, Avonmouth
Bristol BS 11800, UK
Tel-Fax:+44 1179 825961
www.hardingbros.co.uk

Casino Concessionaires

Caesar's Palace at Sea
3570 Las Vegas Blvd. South
Las Vegas, NV 89109, USA
Tel:+1 702-731-7464

Casinos Austria Maritime (CAI)
Emerald Hill Exec. Plaza 2,
4651 Sheridan Str. Suite 303
Hollywood, FL 33021, USA
Telephone in Austria:+43 50-777-50
www.casinos.at

Century Casinos
200-220 East Bennett Ave., PO Box 1006, Cripple Creek, CO 80813, USA
Tel:+1 719-689-9100 Fax:+1 719-689-9700
www.cnty.com

Greater Atlantic Holdings
Casino at Sea, 1001 West Cypress Road
Suite 220, Ft. Lauderdale, FL 33309, USA
Tel:+1 954 491-9291 Fax:+1 954 491-9924
www.casinoatsea.com

Carnival Casinos Corporation
Alton House, 177 High Holborn
London WCIV 7AA, UK
Tel:+44 171-497-0211 Fax:+44 171-240-2573
www.oceancasinojobs.com

International Casino Monitoring Ltd.
PO Box 195 Hythe CT21 6GZ, England
Tel:01303 260108 Fax: 01303 260114
www.intcasmon.ndirect.co.uk

Casinos Austria International
Dr. Karl Lueger Ring, A-1015 Vienna, Austria
Tel:+431 534-40504 Fax:+431 532-9207
www.caicasinos.com

Cruise Staff

Sixth Star Entertainment
21 NW 5th Str. Ft. Lauderdale, FL 33301, USA
Tel:+1 954 462-6760 Fax:+1 954 462-0737
www.sixthstar.com

Ship Services Intern. (SSI)
370 West Camino Gardens Blvd.
Boca Raton, FL 33432, USA
Tel:+1 561 391-5500 Fax:+1 561 450-795
www.richardjoseph.com

Deck and Engineering

Intl. Marine Manning Services
Larkfield House, 14 River Road, Lambeg Lisburn BT27 4SD
Co. Antrim, N. Ireland
Tel:+02890-626215 Fax:+02890-626610
www.internationalmarine.co.uk

Crewfinders International Inc.
404-408 SE 17th Str.
Ft. Lauderdale, FL 33316, USA
Tel:+1 954 522-2739 Fax:+1 954 761-7700
www.crewfinders.com

Humber Ship Services
Carlisle House Carliste Str., Goole
North Humberside DN14 5DS, England
Tel: 01405 767229

V Ships Leisure SAM
Aigue Marine, 24 Avenue de Fontvieille
P.O. Box 639, MC 98013, Monaco
Tel: +44 141 243 2435
Fax: +44 141 243 2436
Only online application
www.vships.com

Denholm Crew Management Ltd.
The Park 107-115 Milton Str.
Glasgow G4 0DN, Scotland
Tel:0141 353 1020 Fax:0141 353 2366
www.denholmship.com

Viking Recruitment
Protea House, Marine Parade

Dover, Kent CT17 9AW, UK
Tel:+44 1304-240881 Fax:+44 1304-240882
www.vikingrecruitment.com

Entertainment Agencies

Bramson Entertainment Bureau
630 Ninth Ave., Suite 203
New York, NY 10036, USA
Tel:+1 212-265-3500 Fax:+1 212-265-6615
www.bramson.com

Bartels Inc.
1740 Elders Mill Road, Senoia, GA 30276, USA
Tel:+1 770-599-6802

Defade Talent Agency
PO Box 2056, Hallandale, FL 33008, USA
Tel:+1 305 932-2986

Jean Ann Ryan Productions
Casting, 308 SE 14th Str.
Ft. Lauderdale, FL 33316, USA
Tel:+1 954 523-6414
www.jeanannryanproductions.com

Neal Hollander Agency, Inc
9936 Majorca Place, Boca Raton
FL 33434, USA
Tel:+1 561 482-1400 Fax:+1 561 479-0035
www.nealhollanderagency.com

Spot Light Entertainment
2121 N. Bayshore Drive, Suite 909
Miami, FL 33137, USA
Tel:+1 305 576-8626

Elaine Avon Ltd.
127 Westhall Road, Warlinghan
Surrey, CR3 9HJ, England
Tel:+44 188 3622317

Showbiz International Cruising Ltd.
Rossall Point, 83 Princess Way Fleetwood
Nr Blackpool Lancs, FY7 8DX, England
Tel:01253-771000 Fax:01253-777711

Garry Brown Associates
27 Downs Side, Cheam
Surrey SM2 7EH, England
Tel:+44 181 6733991 Fax:+44 020 87707241

Matrix Entertainment Ltd.
P.O. Box 70, Oxshott
Surrey KT22 OHS, England

Roger Kendrick Cruising
Entertainment, 6 Orchard Road
St. Annes-on-Sea, Lancs, FY8 1RH, England
Tel:+44 125 3726046 Fax:+44 125 3712125

Stadium Theatre Company
c/o P&O Cruises, Richmond House,
Terminus Terrace, Southampton SO14 3PN Hampshire, England
Tel:+44 1703-534200

Food & Beverage

Apollo Ships Chandlers
1775 NW 70th Ave., Miami, FL 33126, USA
Tel:+1 305 592-8790 Fax:+1 305 593-8335
www.apolloship.com

Apollo Ships Chandlers
VIP International, 17 Charing Cross Road
GB- London WC2 OEP, England
www.vipinternational.co.uk

Seachest Associates
3655 NW 87th Ave., Miami, FL 33178, USA
Tel:+1 305 599-2600
www.carnival.com

Global Ship Services
Bayside Office Center
245 S.E 1st Street, Suite 332
Miami, Fl 33131, USA
Tel:+1 305 374-8649 Fax:+1 305 374-4342
www.globalshipservices.com

Triton Cruise Services, Inc.
1007 N. America Way, Suite 407
Miami, FL 33132, USA
Tel:+1 305 358-7860 Fax:+1 305 374-3931
www.cruisecatering.com

Renard International
1212x Richard Str. West, Suite 500
Toronto, Ontario M5H 2K1, Canada
www.renard-international.com

V Ships Leisure SAM
Aigue Marine, 24 Avenue de Fontvieille
P.O. Box 639, MC 98013, Monaco
Tel : +44 141 243 2435
Fax : +44 141 243 2436
only online application
www.vships.com

Gentlemen Hosts

The Working Vacation, Inc.
The Gentlemen Host Program, 12544 West 159 Str. Lockport, IL 60441, USA
Tel:+1 708 301-7535 Fax:+1 708 301-6202
www.theworkingvacation.com

To Sea with Z
19195 Mystic Point Drive, Tower 100
Suite 2007, Aventura, FL 33180, USA
Tel:+1 305-931-1026 Fax:+1 305-931-1026
www.toseawithz.com

Gift Shop/Retail Sales

Starboard Cruise Services, Inc.
8052 NW 14th Str., Miami, FL 33126, USA
Tel:+1 786 845-7300 Fax +1 305 593-0545
www.starboardcruise.com

Harding Brothers
Avonmouth Way, Avonmouth
Bristol BS 11800, UK
Tel-Fax:+44 1179 825961
www.hardingbros.co.uk

Lecturer and Instructors

Program Experts, Inc.
PO Box 510, Cresskill, NJ 07626, USA
Tel:+1 201 569-7950

Abarta Media
11900 Biscayne Blvd., Suite 300
Miami, FL 33181, USA
Tel: +1305 892-6644 Fax:+1305 892-1005

Medical Agencies

Use the official postal addresses of Carnival,
Celebrity, Disney, Holland America and Norwegian cruise lines.

American College for Emergency Medicine
PO Box 619911
Dallas TX 75261-9911, USA
Tel:+1 972-550-0911 Fax:+1 972-580-2816
www.acep.org

Cunard Line Ltd.
Medical Department, Southwestern House
Canute Road Southampton SO14 3NR
Hampshire, England
Tel:+44 17037-16582
www.cunard.com

Royal Caribbean International
Harbitzalleen Legesenter, PO Box
340 Skoyen, 0212 Oslo, Norway
Tel:+47 2273-4611 Fax:+47 2273-144

Musical Floor Show Producers

Jean Ann Ryan Productions
Casting, 308 SE 14th Str.
Ft. Lauderdale, FL 33316, USA
Tel:+1 954 523-6414
www.jeanannryanproductions.com

Basa Productions
Suite C, 67A High Str., Walton-on-Themes, Surrey K12 1DJ, England
Tel-Fax:01932 240038

Kennedy Entertainment
244 South Academy Str.
Mooresville NC 28115, USA
Tel:+1 704 662-3501 Fax:+1 704 662-3668

Photography

Image Photo Services
Beacon Centre, Suite A, 2085 NW 87th Ave. Miami, FL 33172, USA
Tel:+1 305 476-3666 Fax:+1 305 476-36663
www.image.com

Image Photo Services
Long Photographic Svcs, P.O. Box 466
Woking, Surrey GU21 3YG, England
Tel-Fax:+44 1483-451584
www.imageservices.com

Ocean Images
Shipboard Services Ltd.
PO Box 621 Le Gallais Chambers 54 Bath Str.
St. Helier. Jersey JE4 8YD, Channel Islands
Tel:+1 954 523-2308 Fax:+1 954 527-4262
www.ocean-images.com

Ocean Images
7 Home Farm Business Centre, Lockerley
Romsey, Hampshire, SO51 OJT, England
Tel:+44 1794 341415
www.ocean-images.com

Trans-Ocean Photo Service
New York Passenger, Pier 8, 711-12th Ave.
Suite 1, New York, NY 10019, USA
Tel:+1 212 757-2707 Fax:+1 212 265-6943
www.transoceanphotos.com

Ocean Pictures
Canefield Farmhouse, Lockerley,
Hampshire, SO51 OJH, England
Tel:+44 179-4342424

Neptune Photographic
202 Fulham Road, London SW10 9NB, England
Tel:020 7351-7181

Recruiting Agencies

Apollo Ships Chandlers
1775 NW 70th Ave., Miami, FL 33126, USA
Tel:+1 305 592-8790 Fax:+1 305 593-8335
www.apolloship.com

CTI Group
Dept. WP2, 1535 SE 17th Str., Suite 206
Ft. Lauderdale, FL 33316, USA
Tel:+1 954 728-9975 Fax:+1 954 728-9697
www.cti-usa.com

Blue Seas
Online application at www.jobxchange.com

Seafarer Association
7 Berkley Crescent, Gravesend
Kent DA 12 2AH, England
Tel: 01474 329990 Fax: 01474 329995
www.seafarassociates.co.uk

Intl. Cruise Management Agency
Jernbanetorget 4B, P.O. Box 95,
Sentrum N-0154, Oslo, Norway
Tel:+47 23 357000 Fax:+47 23 357001
www.icma.no

Buro Metro
PO Box 626, Ch-8039, Zurich, Switzerland
Tel:+1201 4110

Sea Sources Inc.
Moelkhofgasse 3 T.7, 5020 Salzburg, Austria
Tel:+43 662 849786 Fax:+43 662 849210

International Services
Boite Postale 23, 91250 Str.
St. Germain Les Corbeils, France
Tel:+33 160 759595 Fax:+33 160 759797
www.internationalservices.fr

Proship Entertainment
5253 Decarie Blvd., Suite 308
Montreal, Quebec H3W 3C2, Canada
www.proship.com

Cruise Service International
601 Dundas Str. West, P.O. Box 24070
Whitby, Ontario L1N 8X8, Canada

Security and Firefighters

International Maritime Securities
The Garden House, Little Chilmington
Ashford, Kent TN23 3DN, England
Tel:+44 1233-643805 Fax:+44 1233-635290
www.intmarsec.co.uk

Printed in the United Kingdom
by Lightning Source UK Ltd.
121342UK00003B/38/A